With Special Thanks
and Smiles to
my sister Petra,
Connie & Ken
& Marc Beattie

:-)

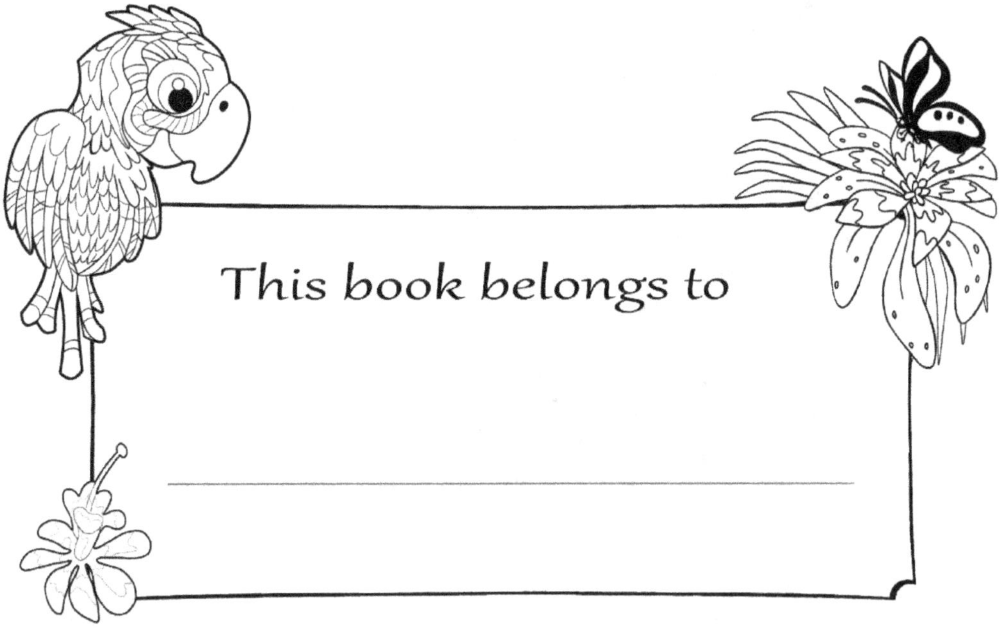
This book belongs to

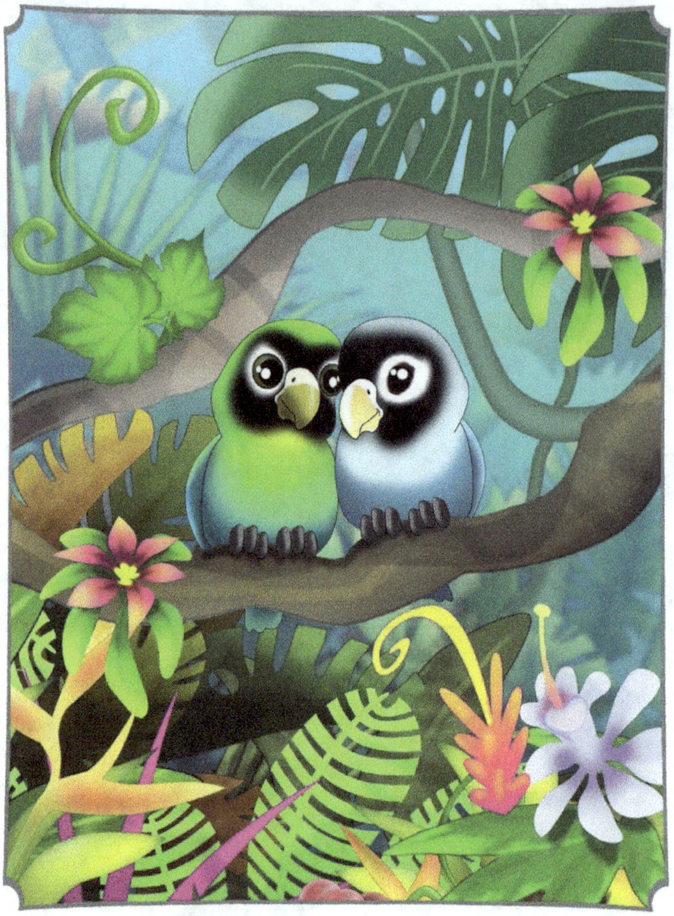

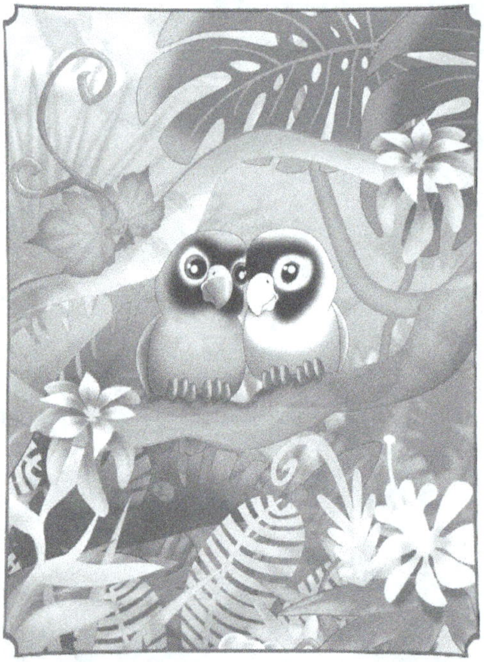

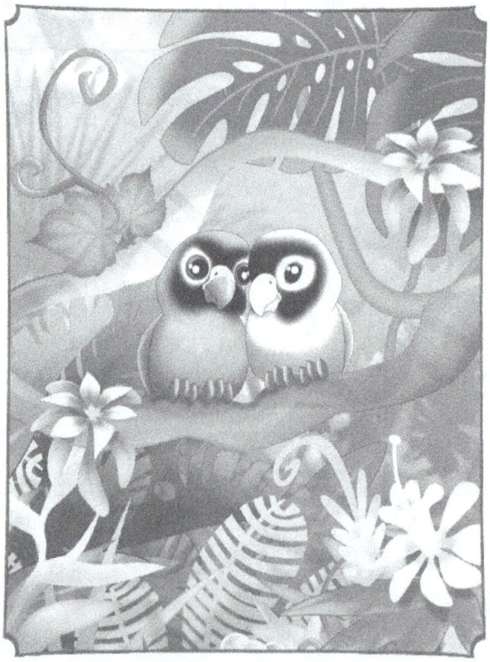

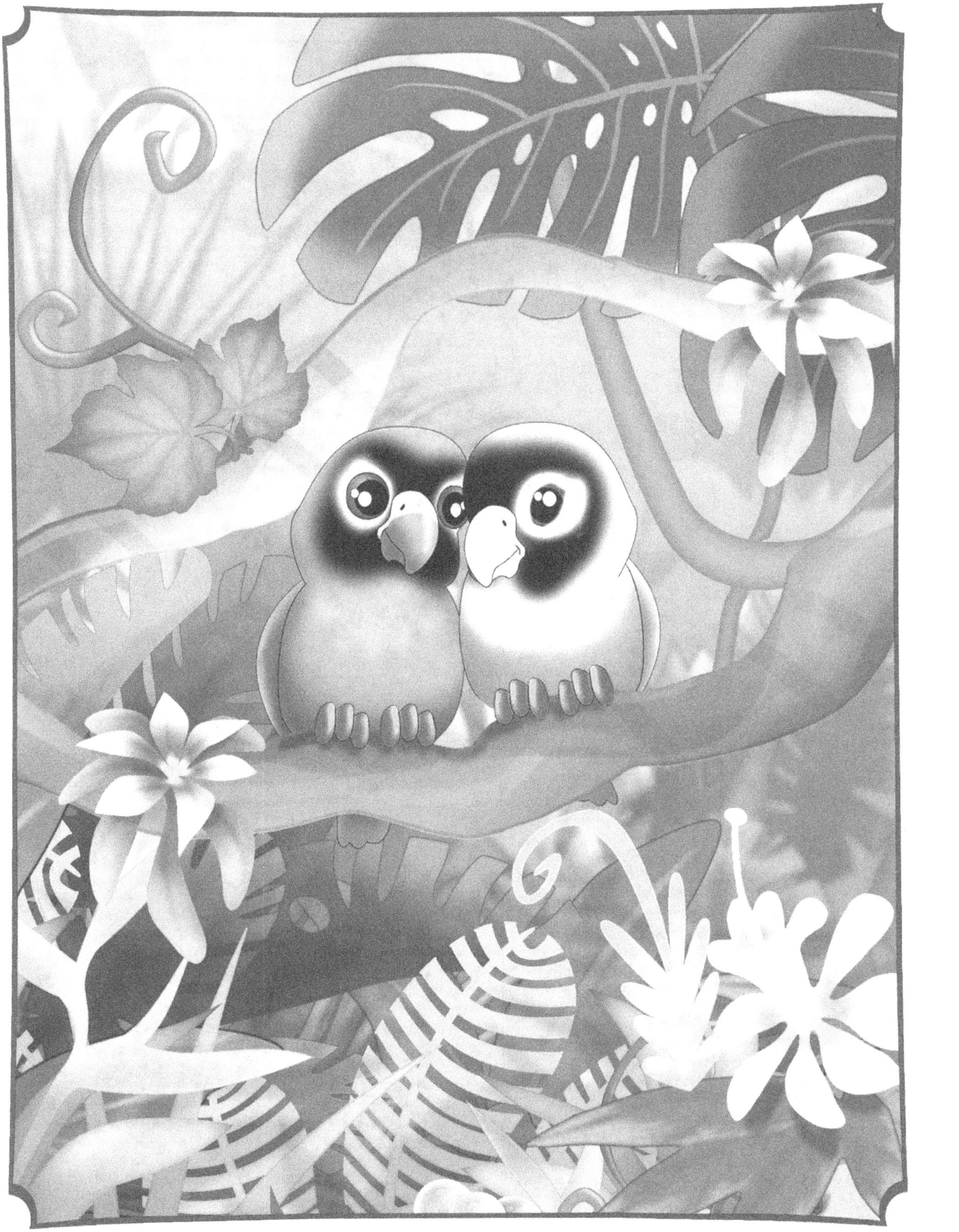

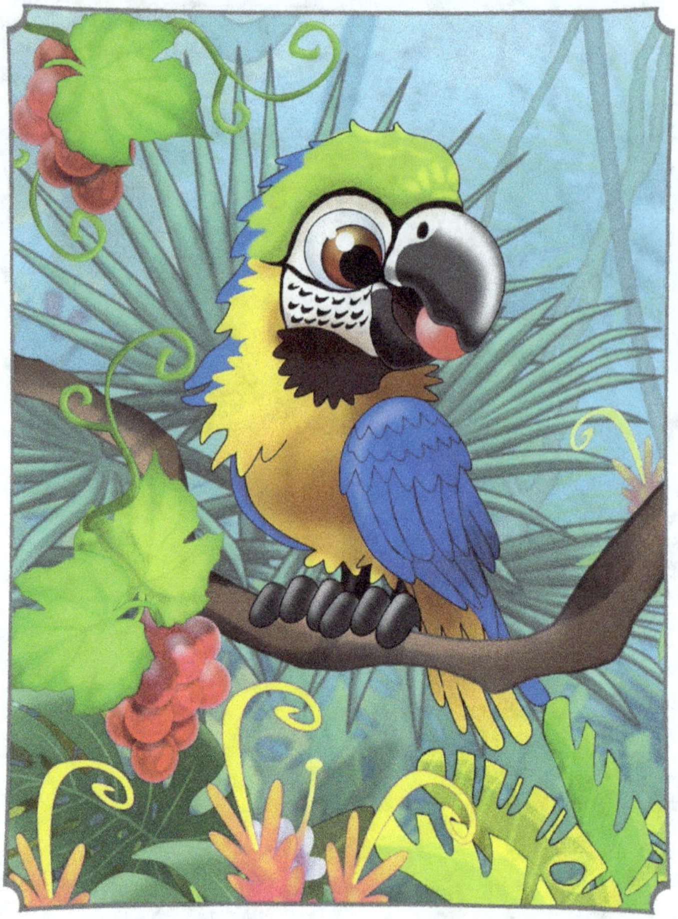
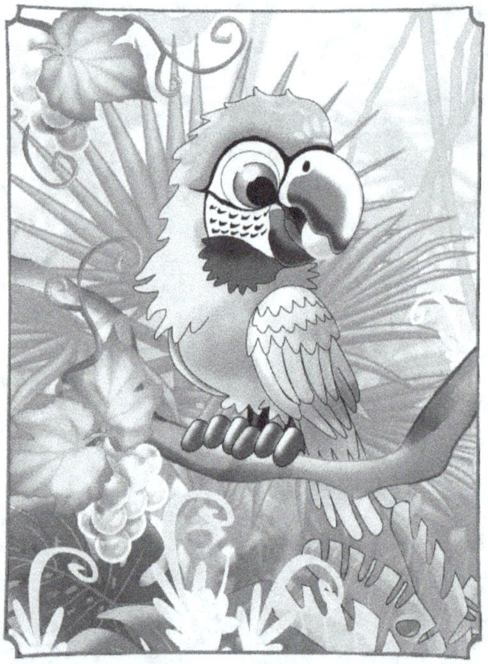
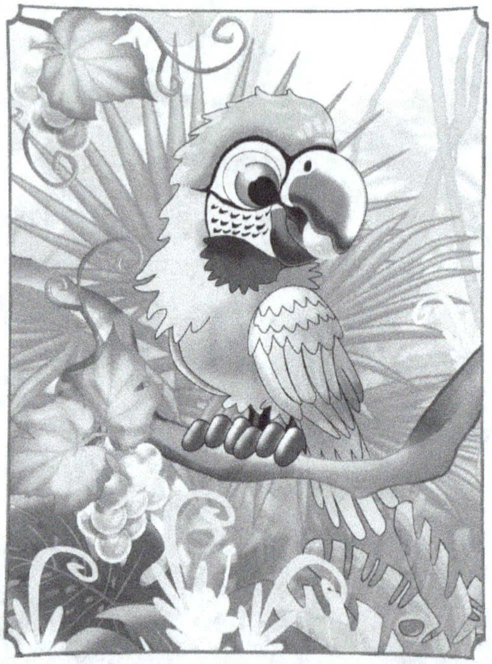

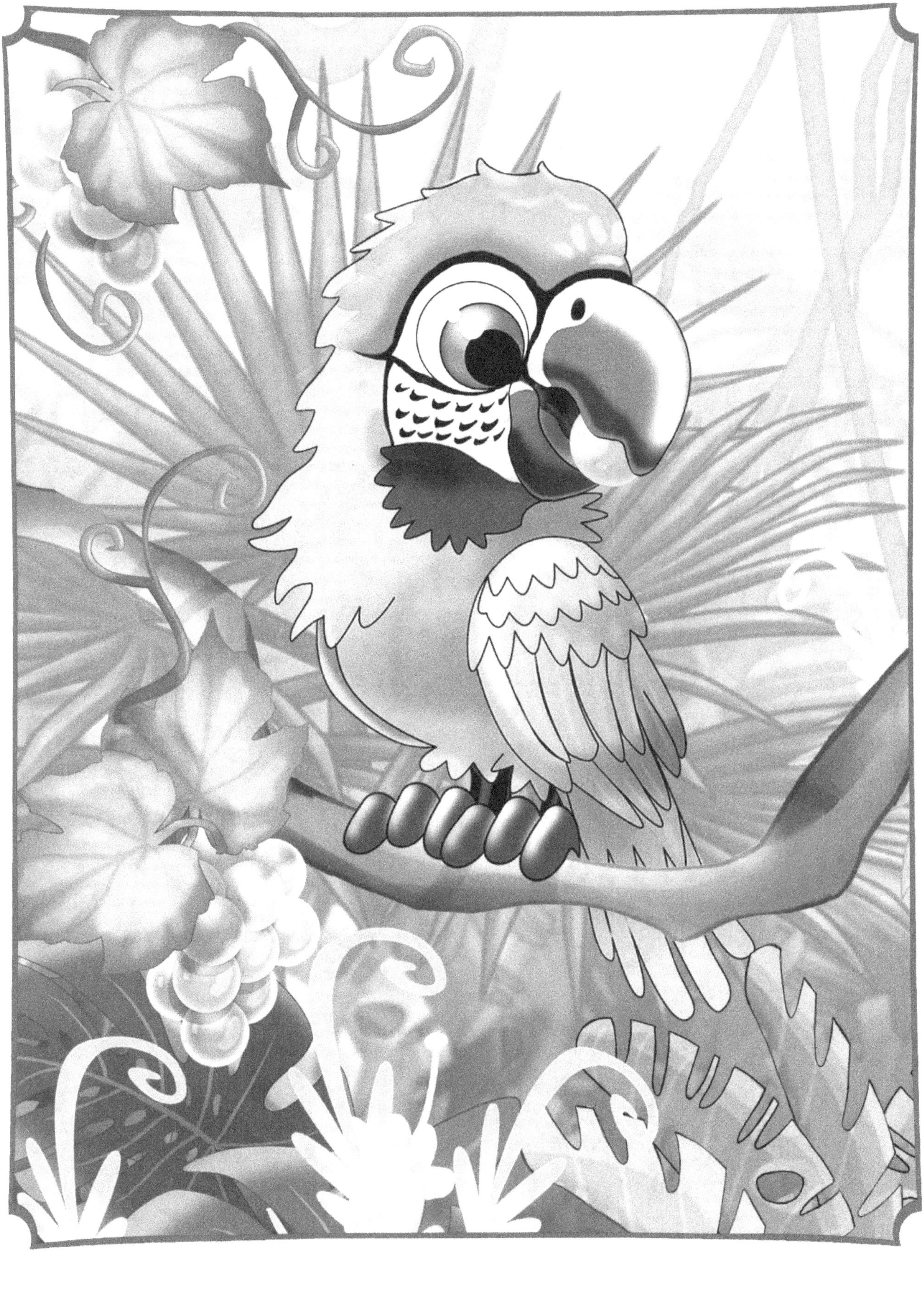

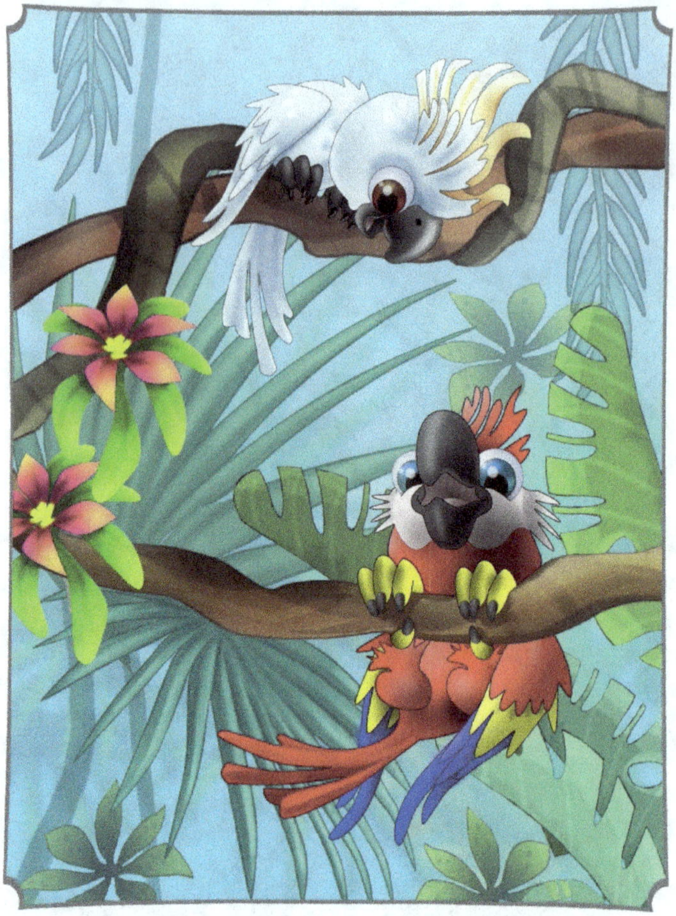
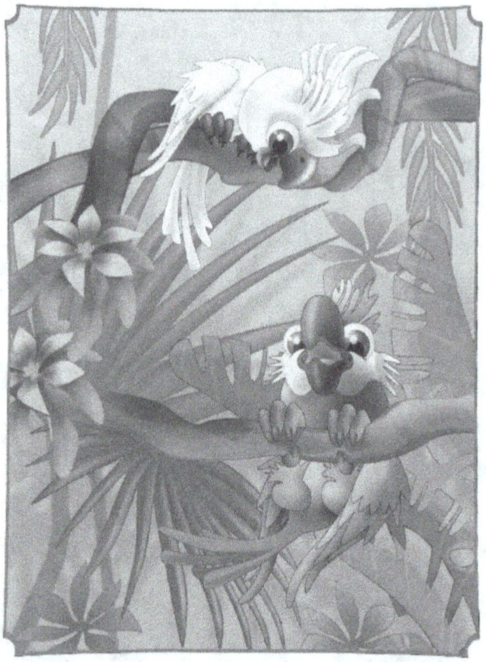
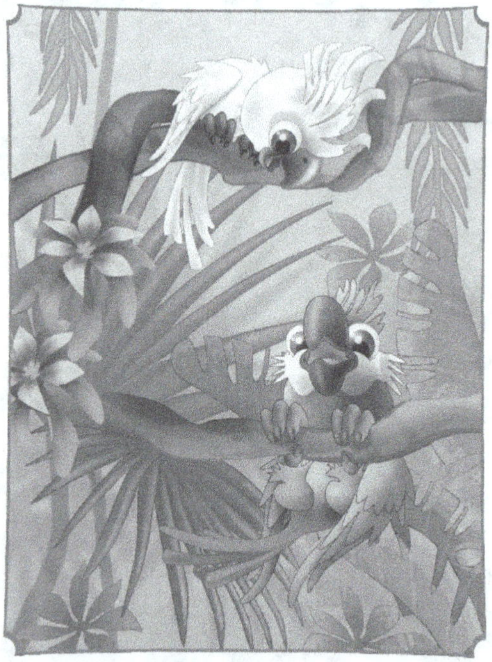

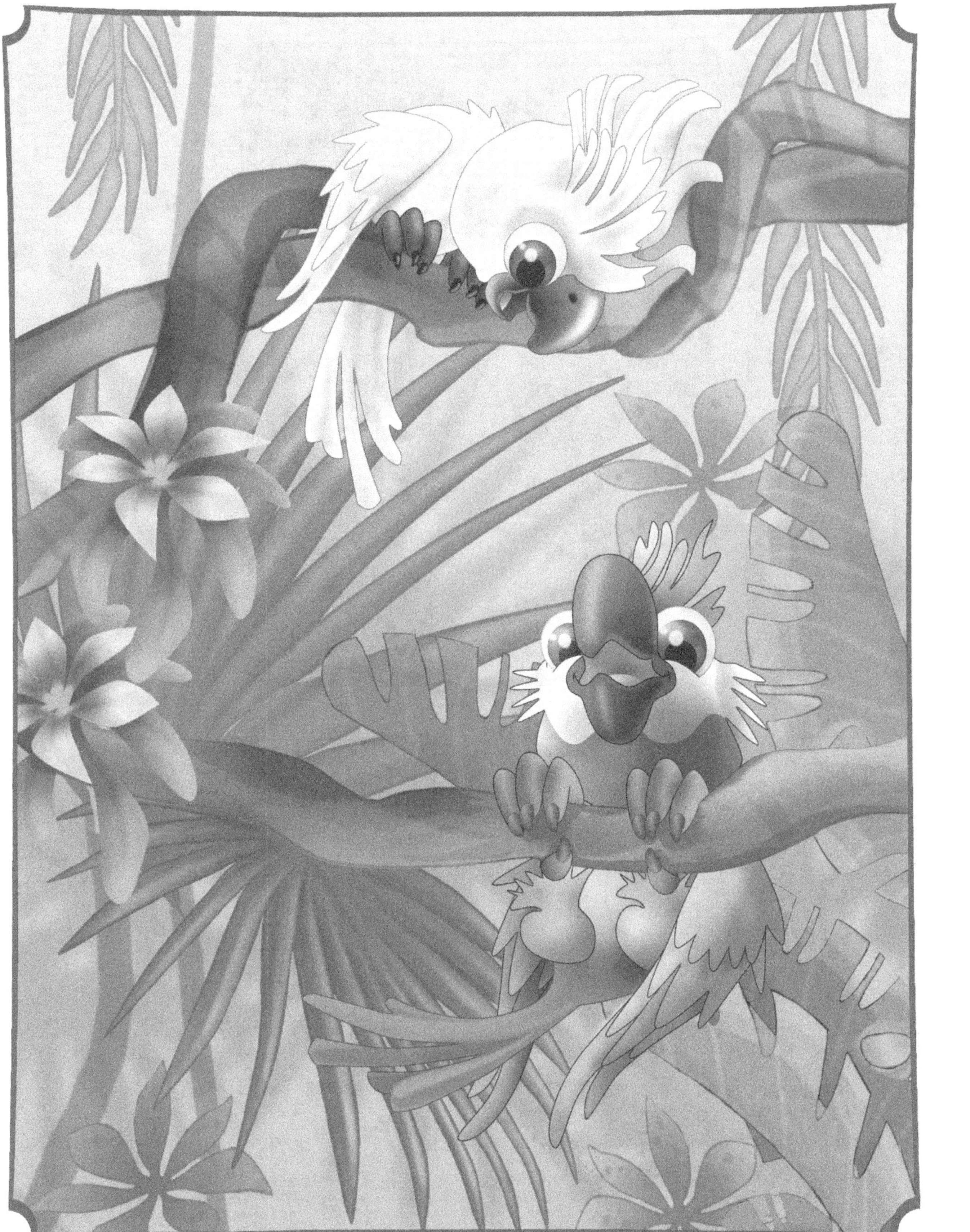

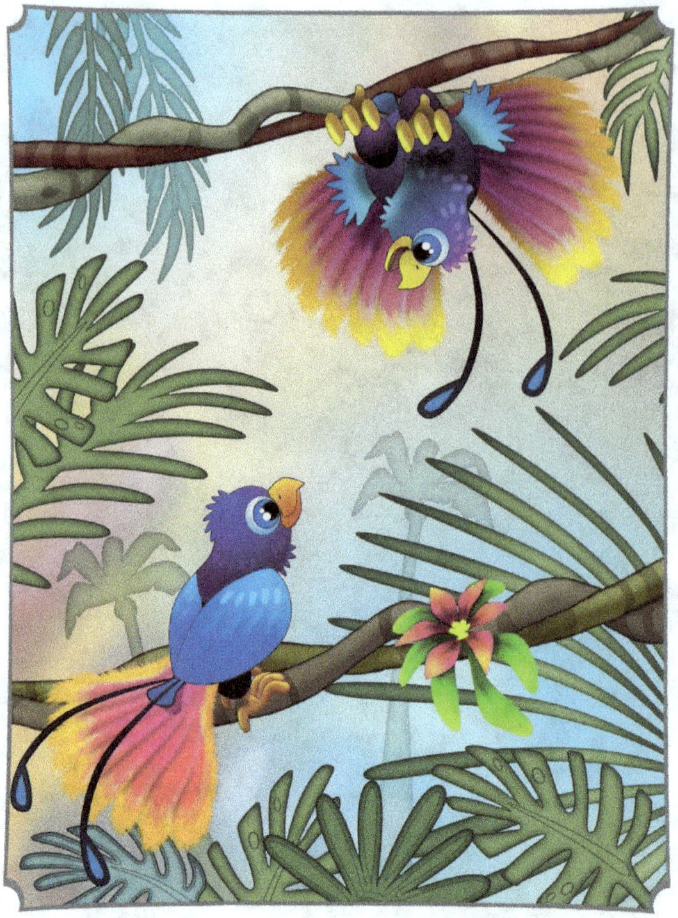

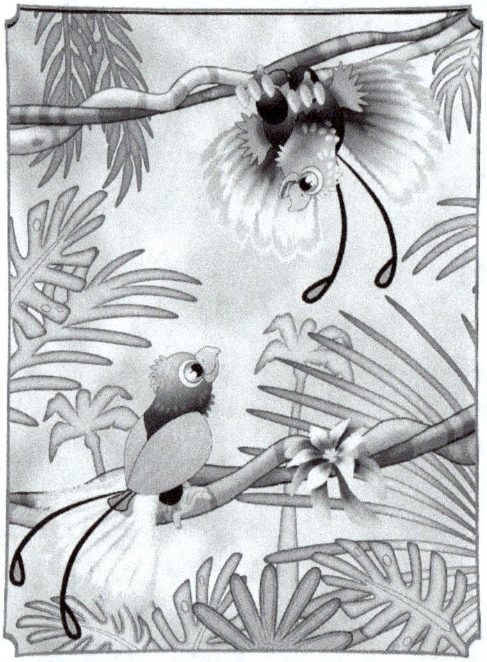

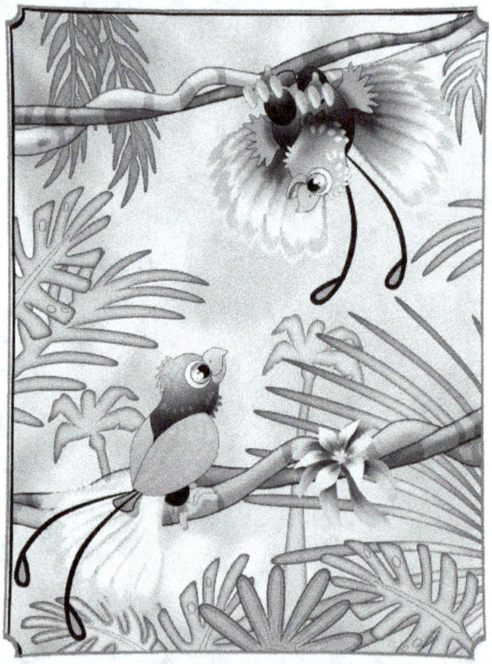

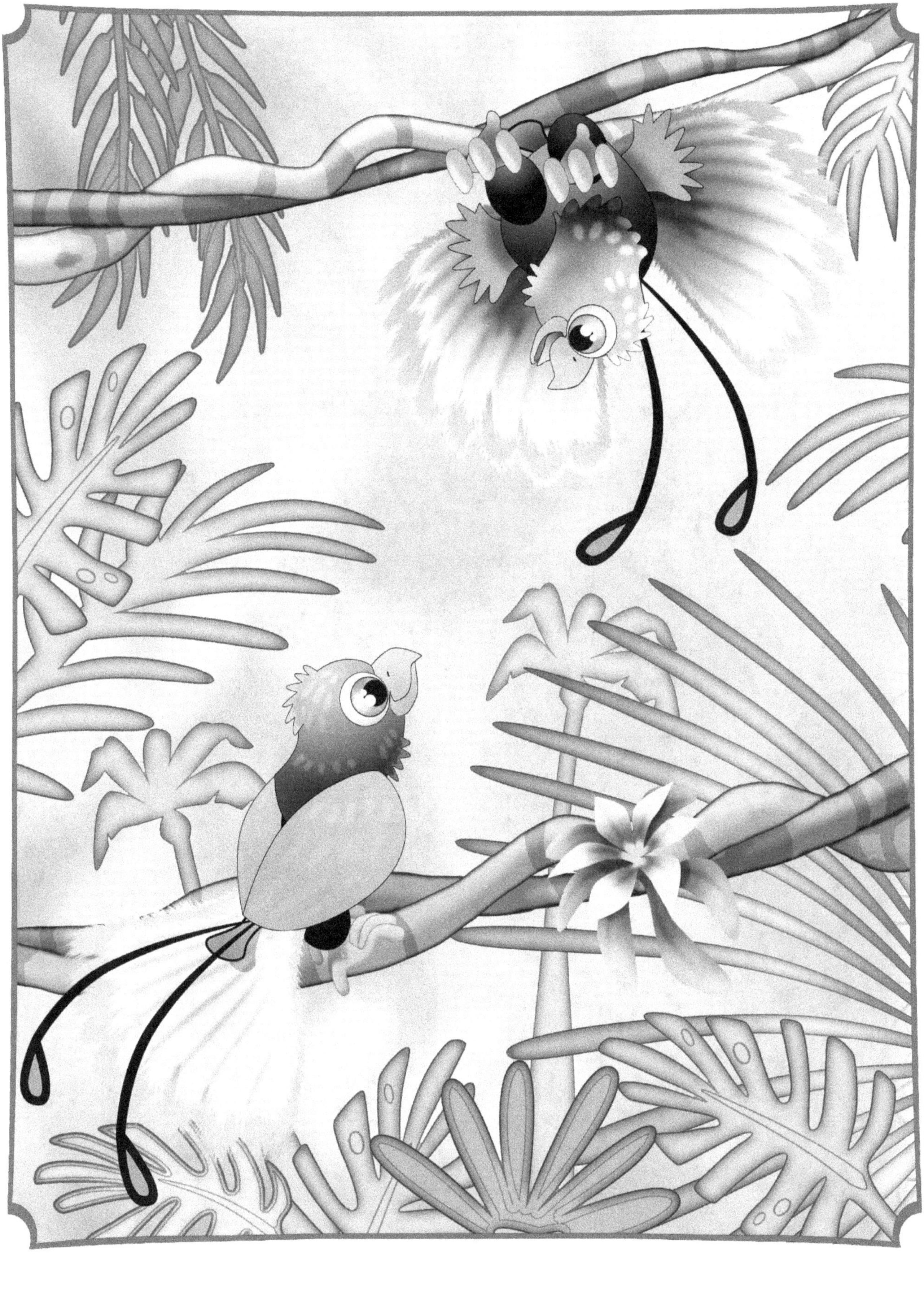

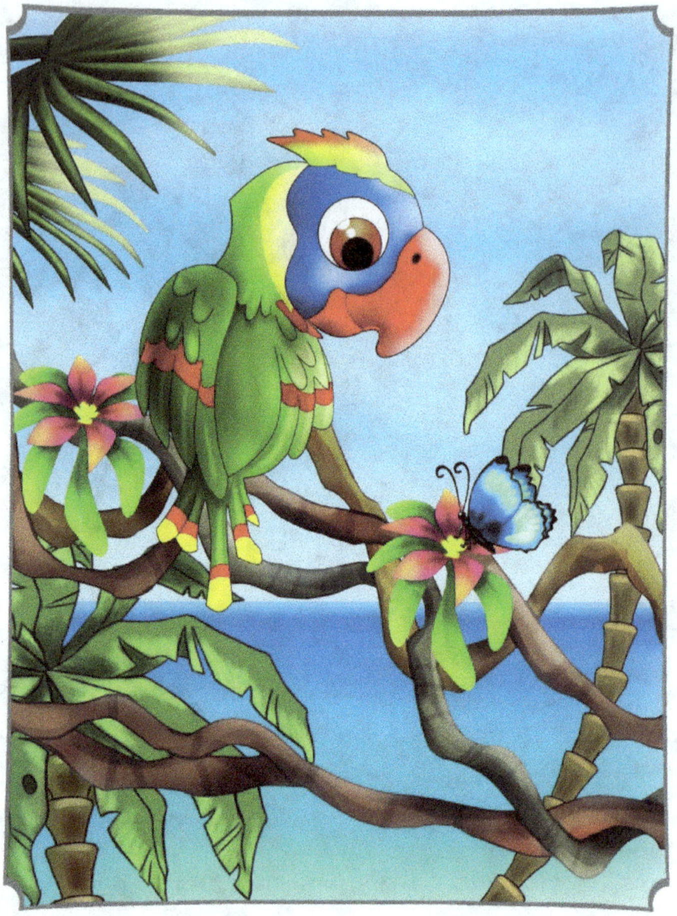

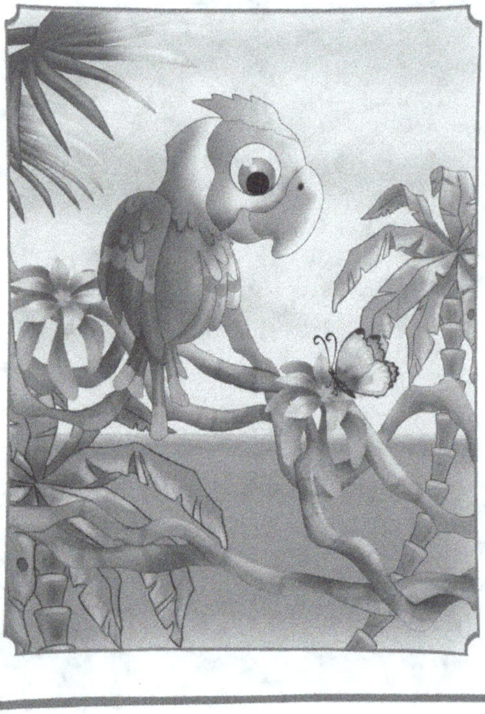

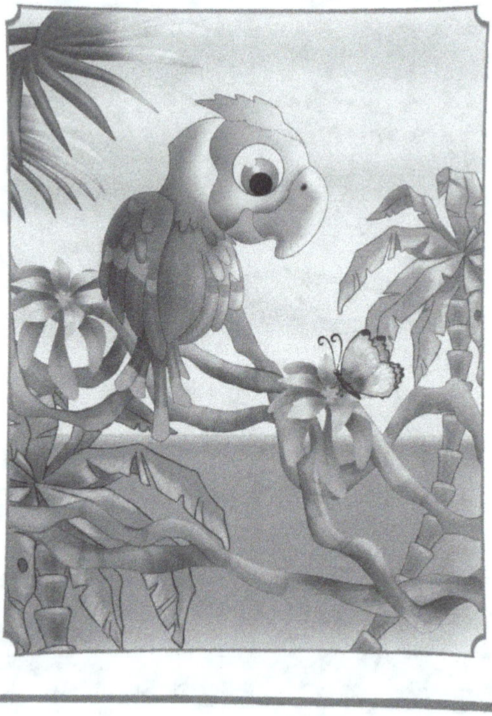

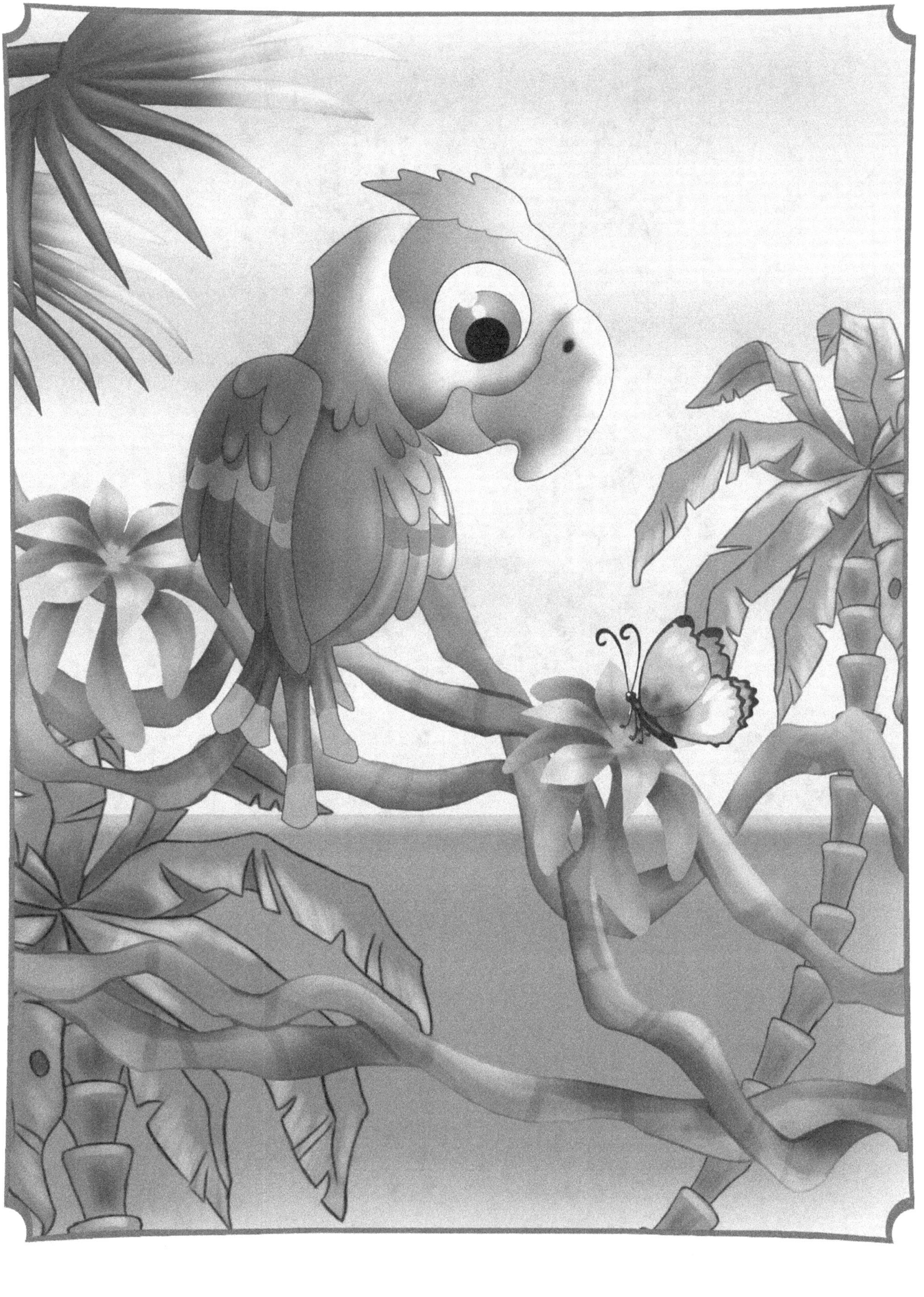

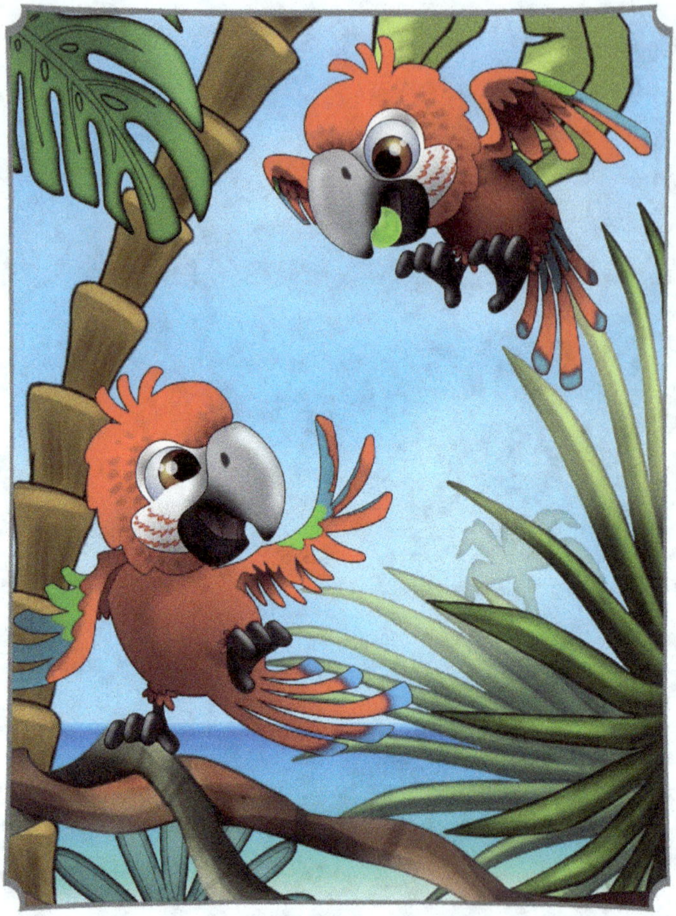

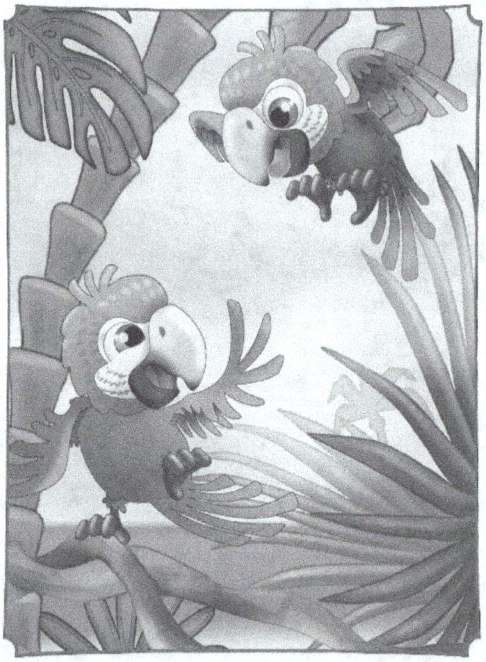

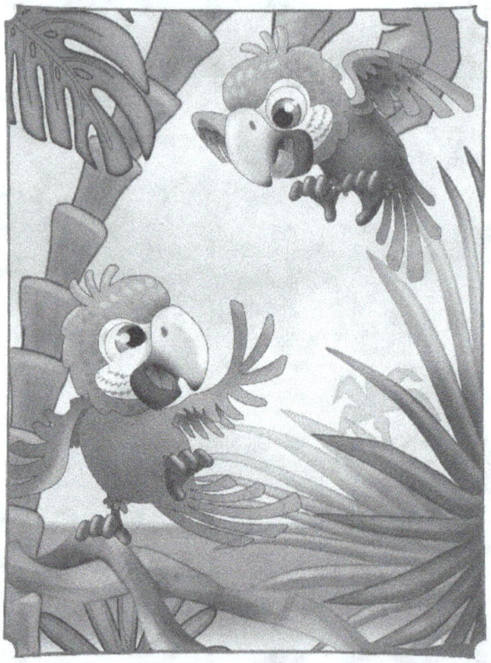

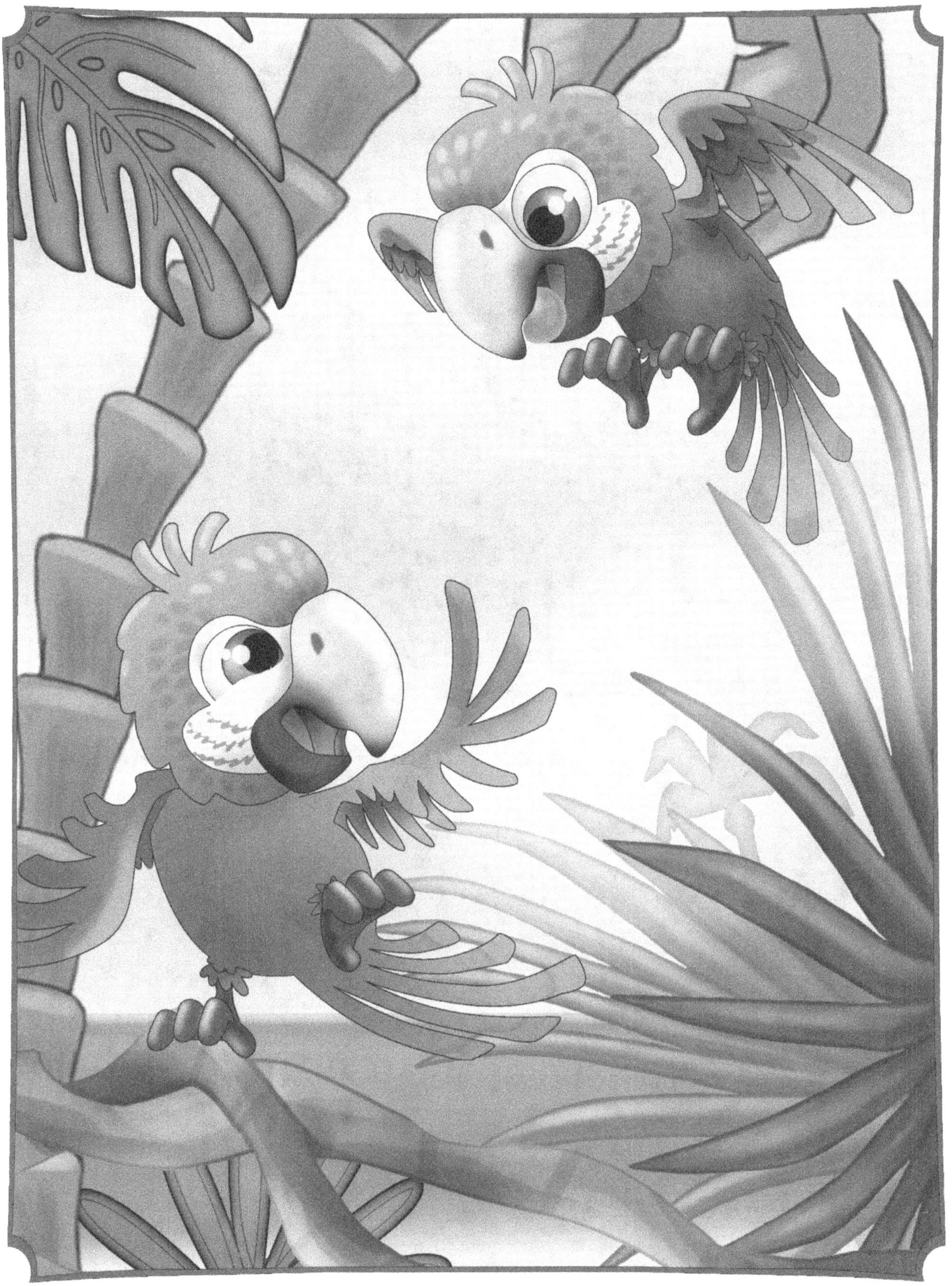

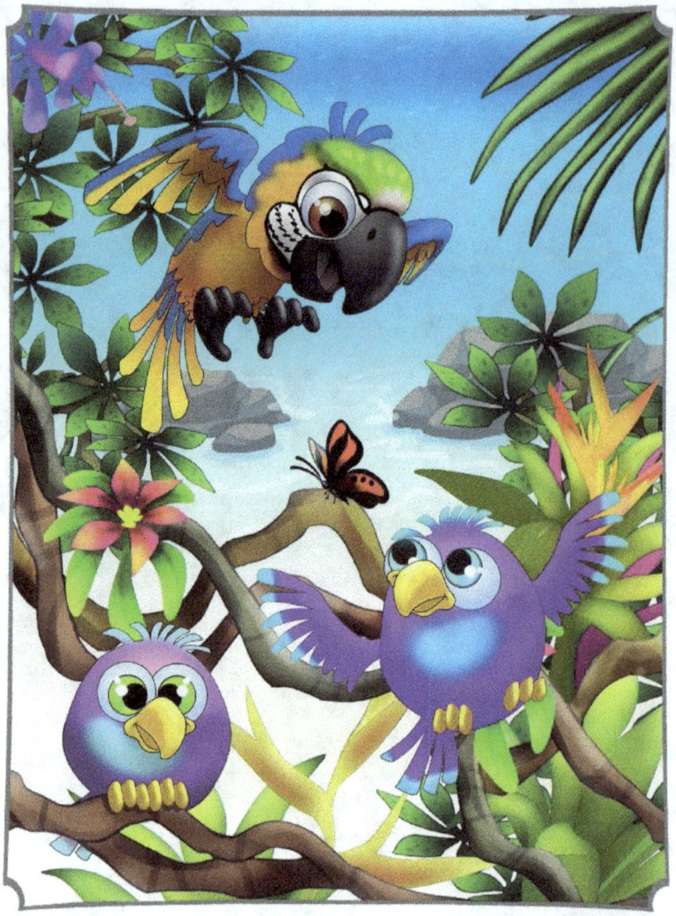

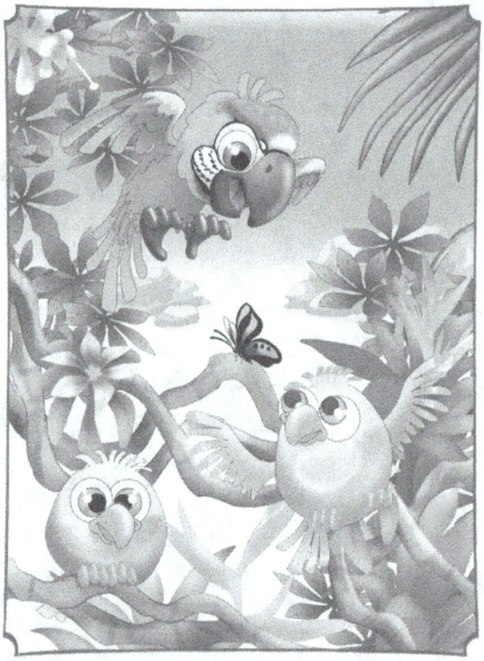

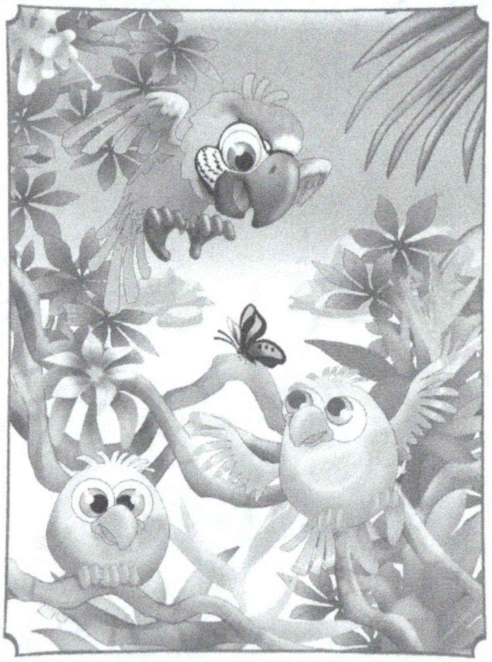

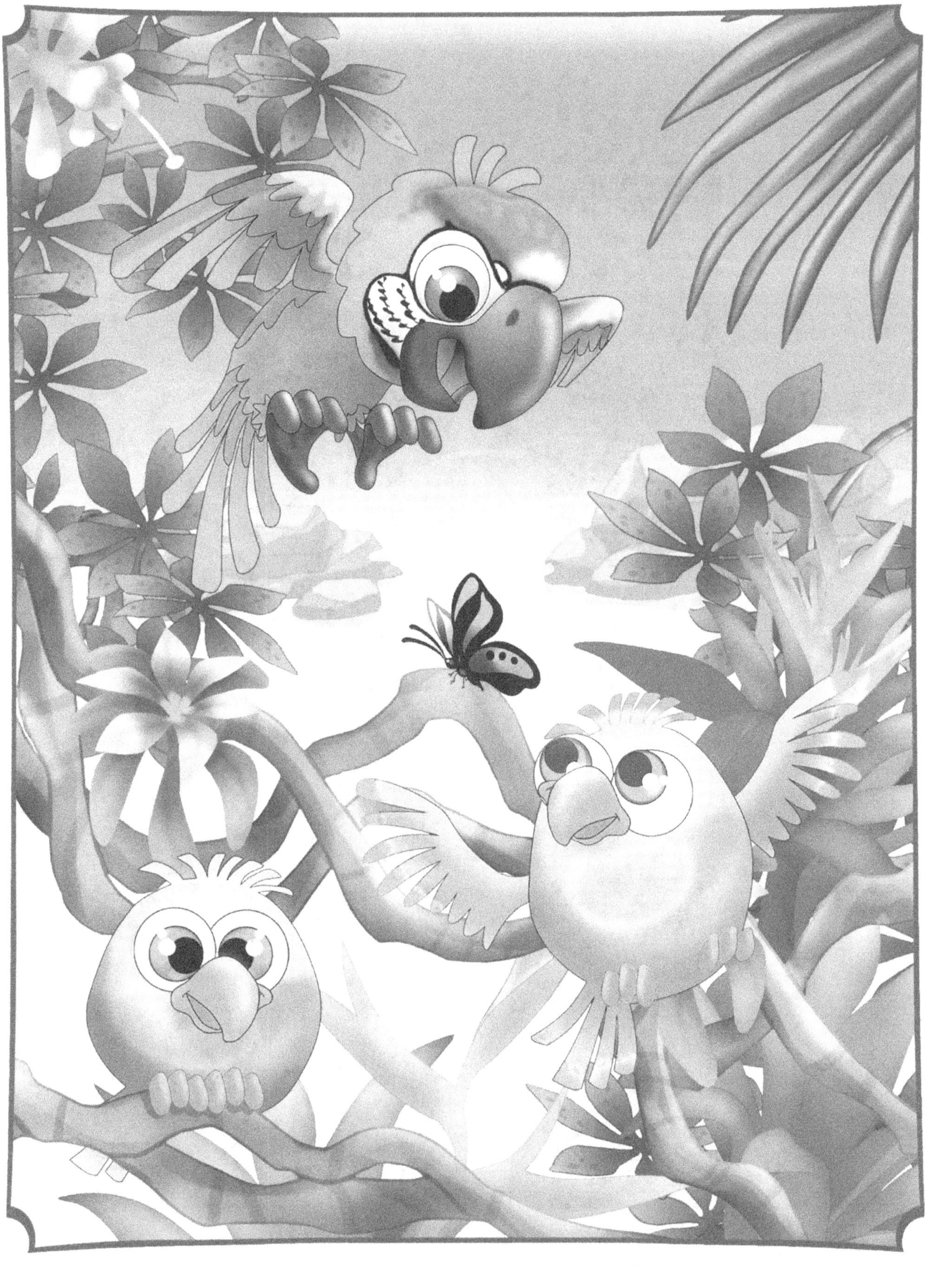

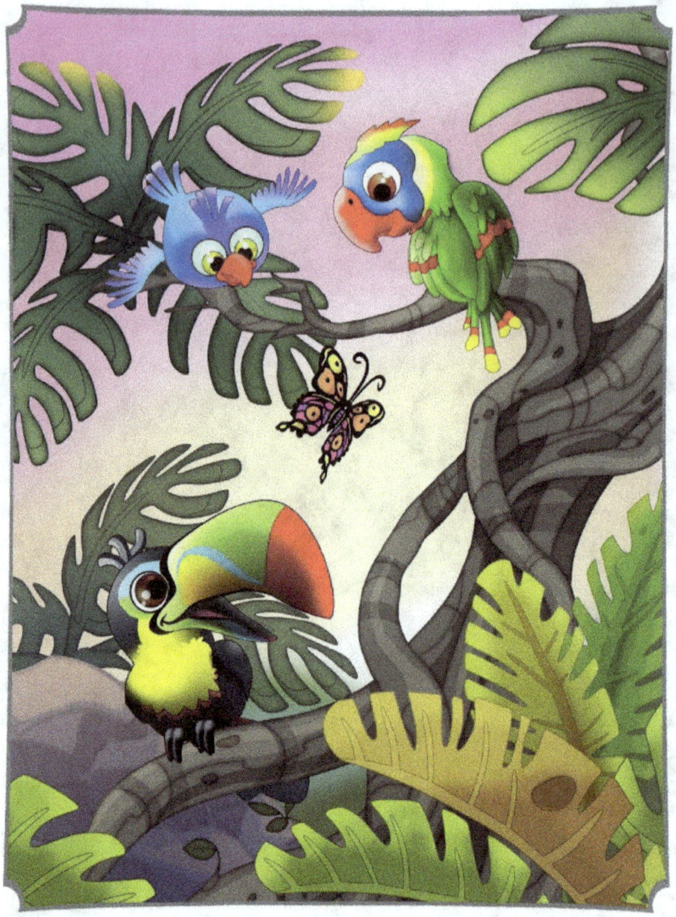

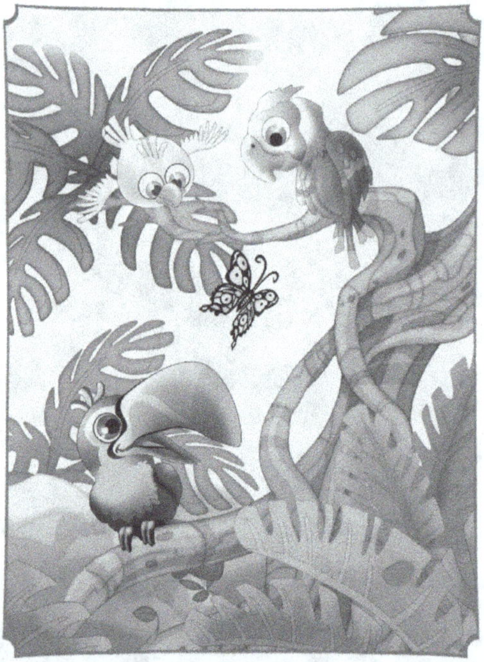

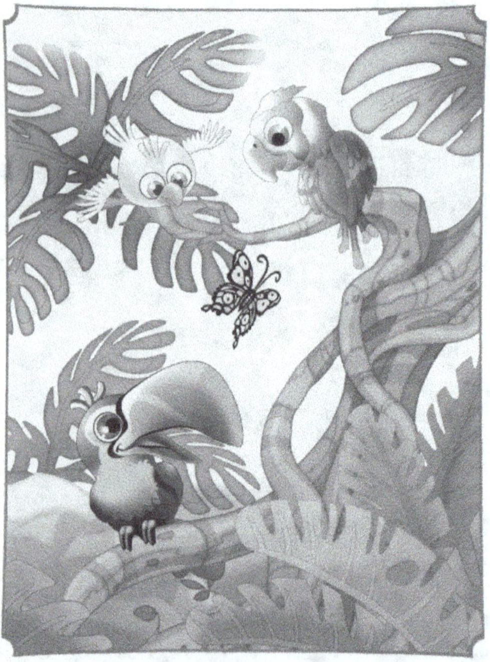

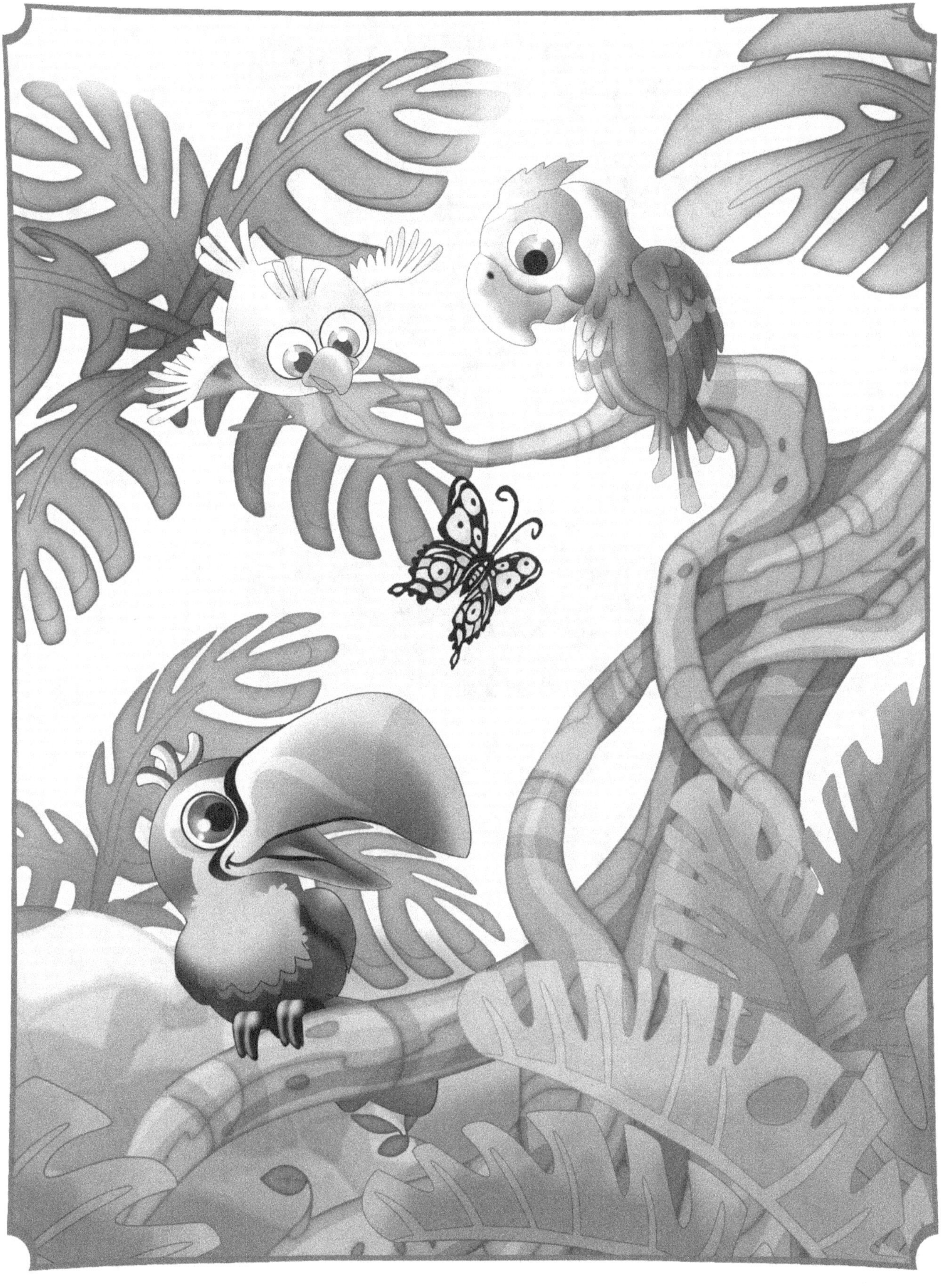

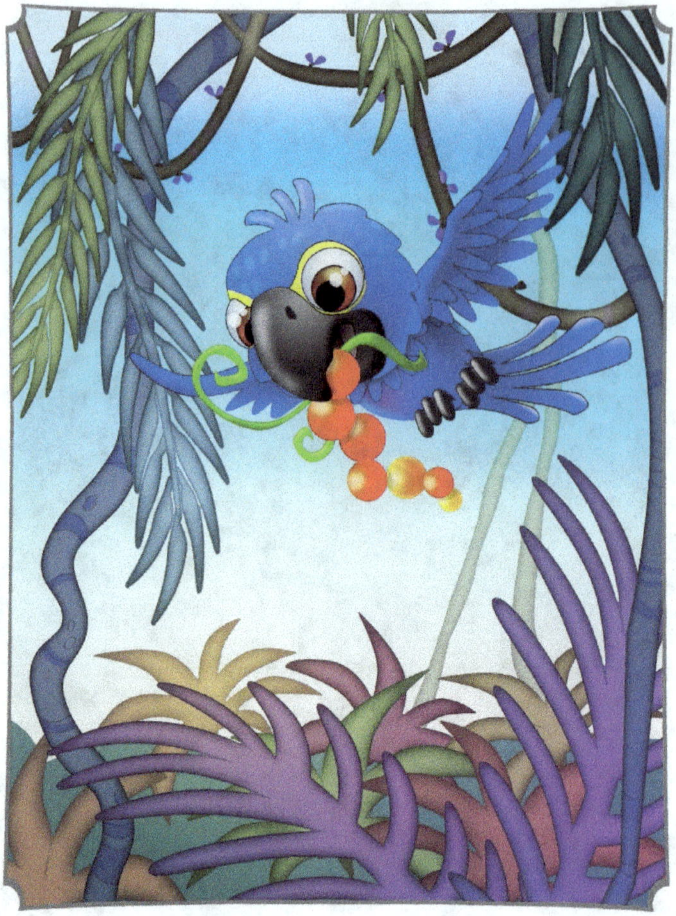

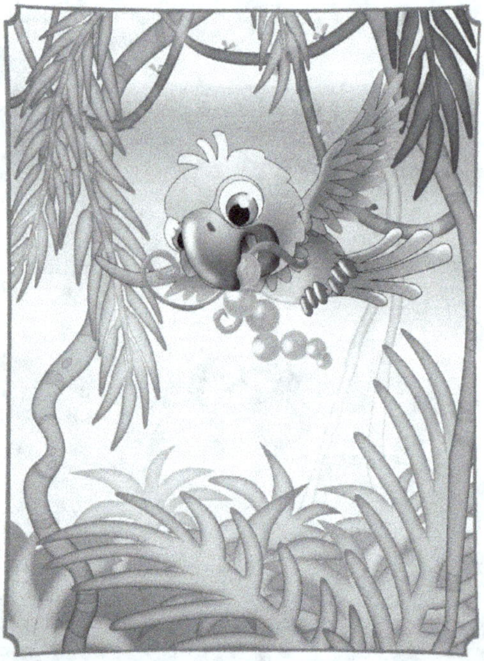

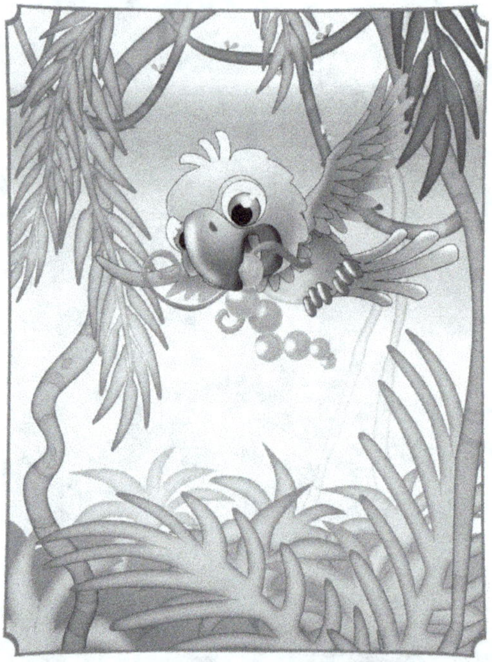

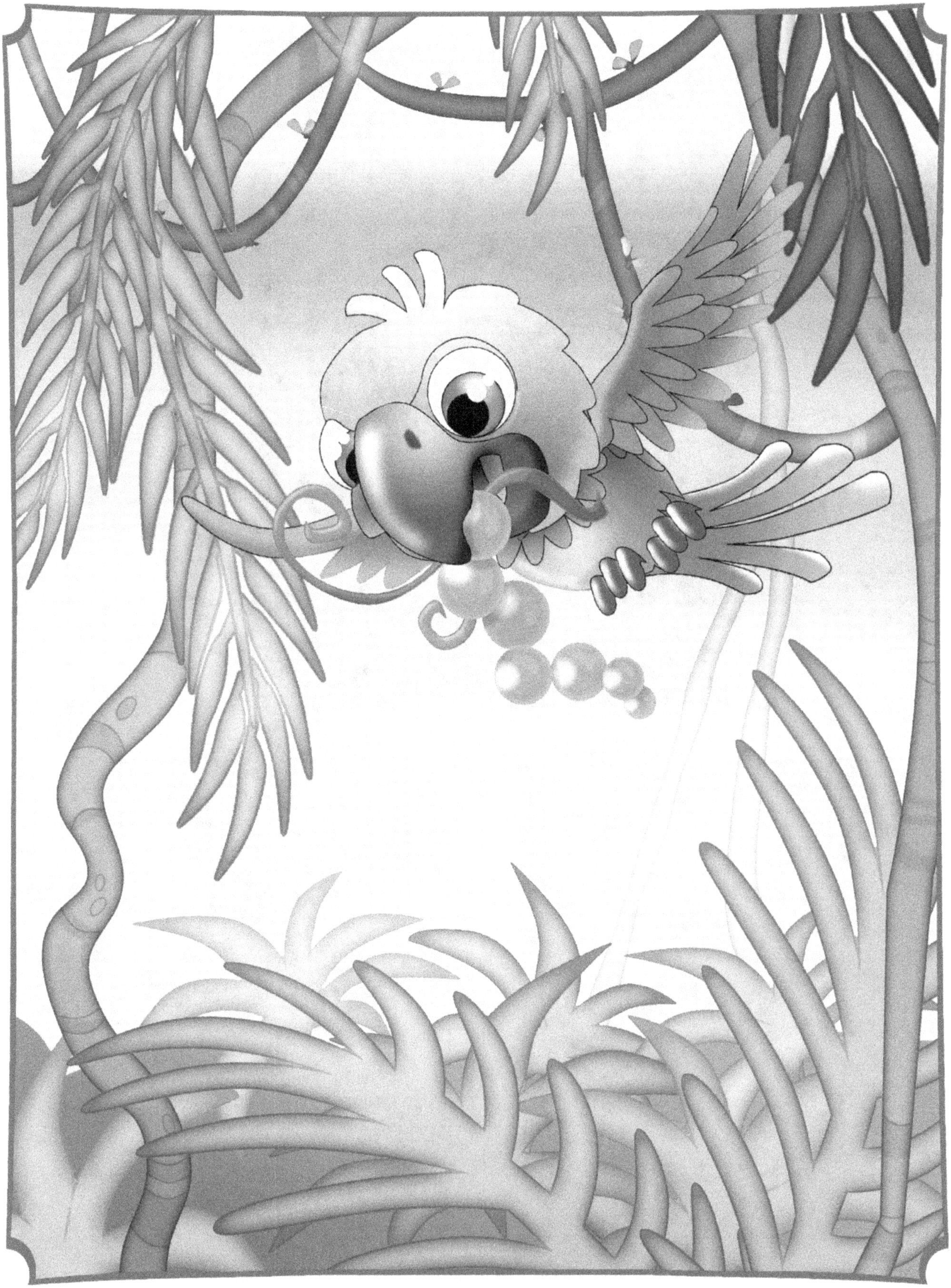

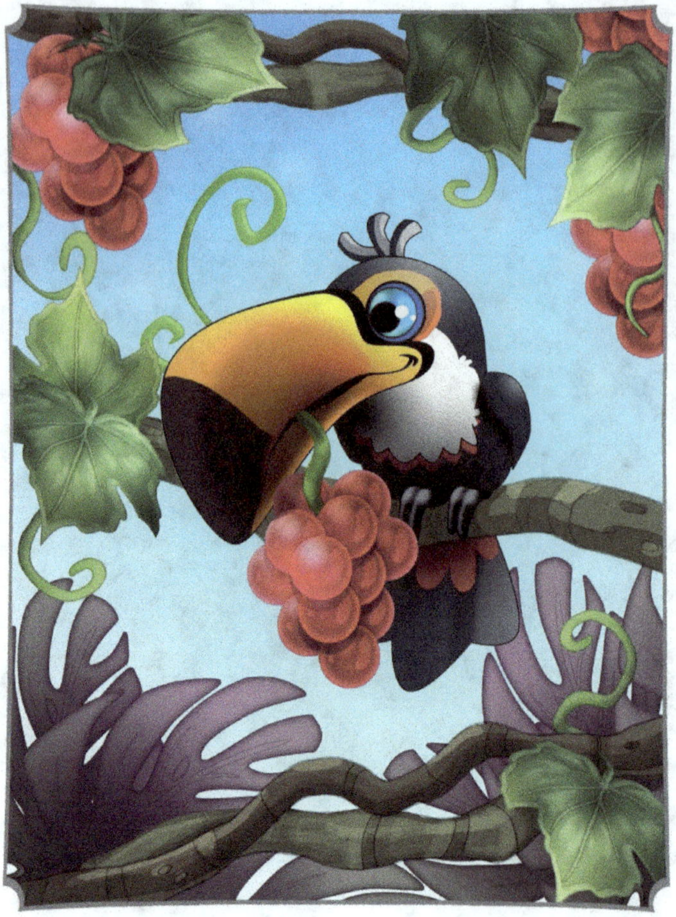

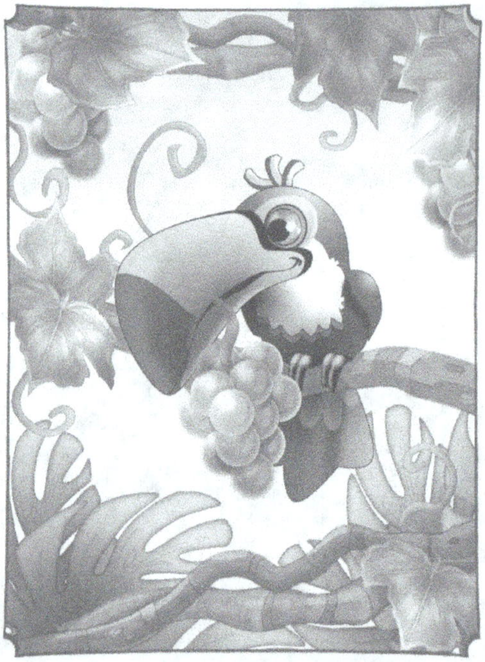

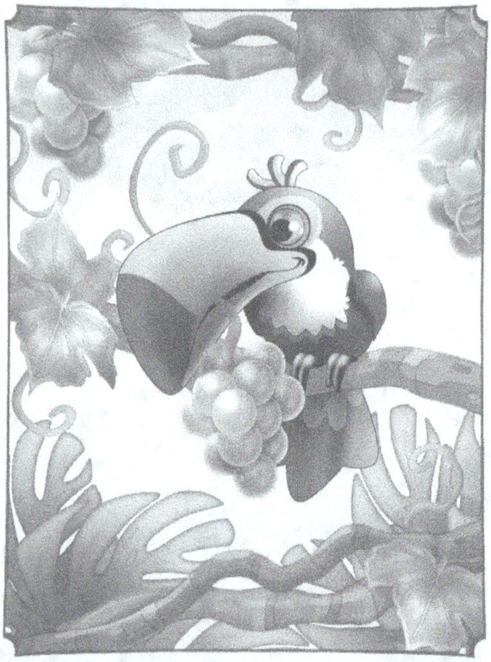

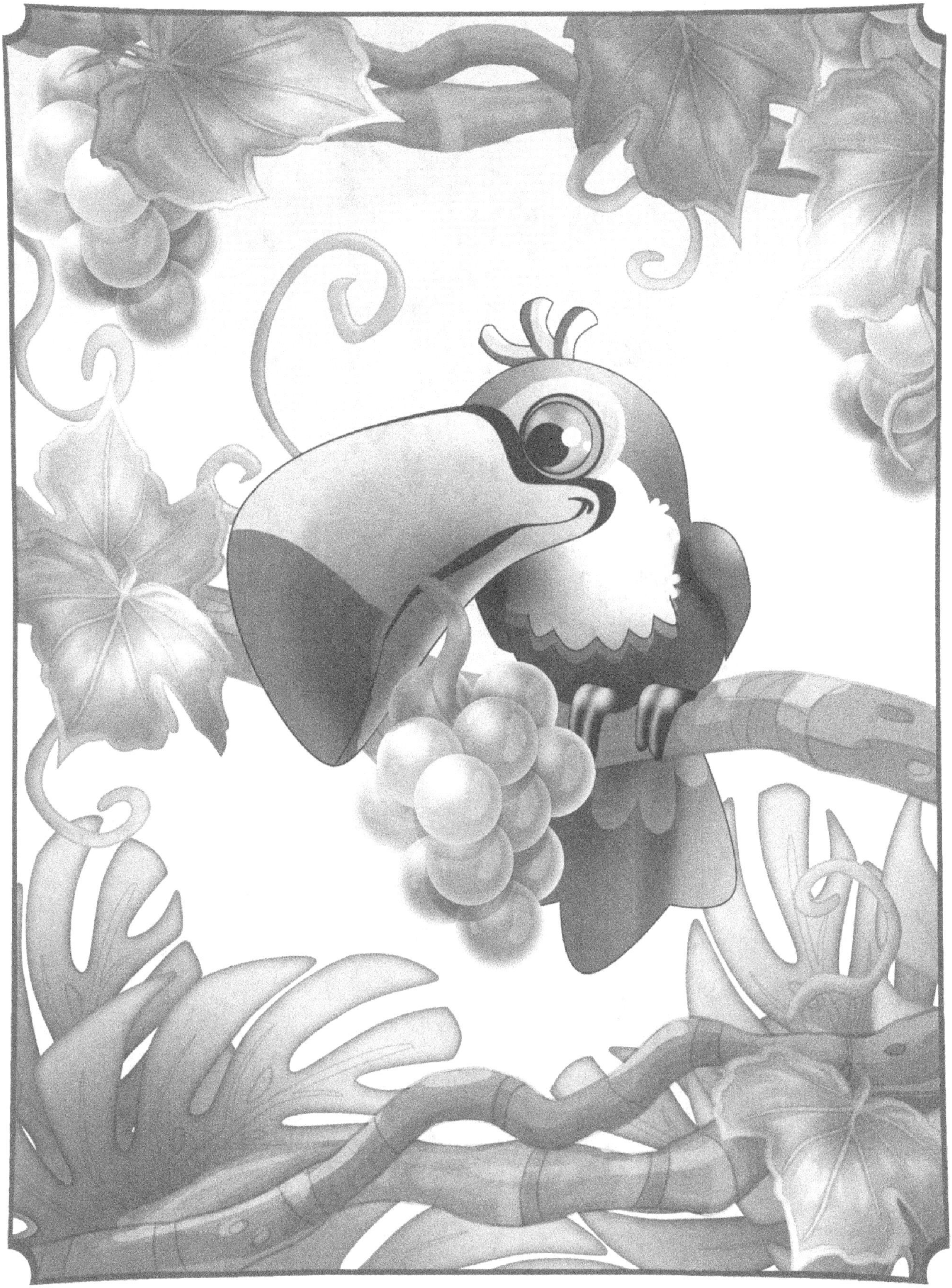

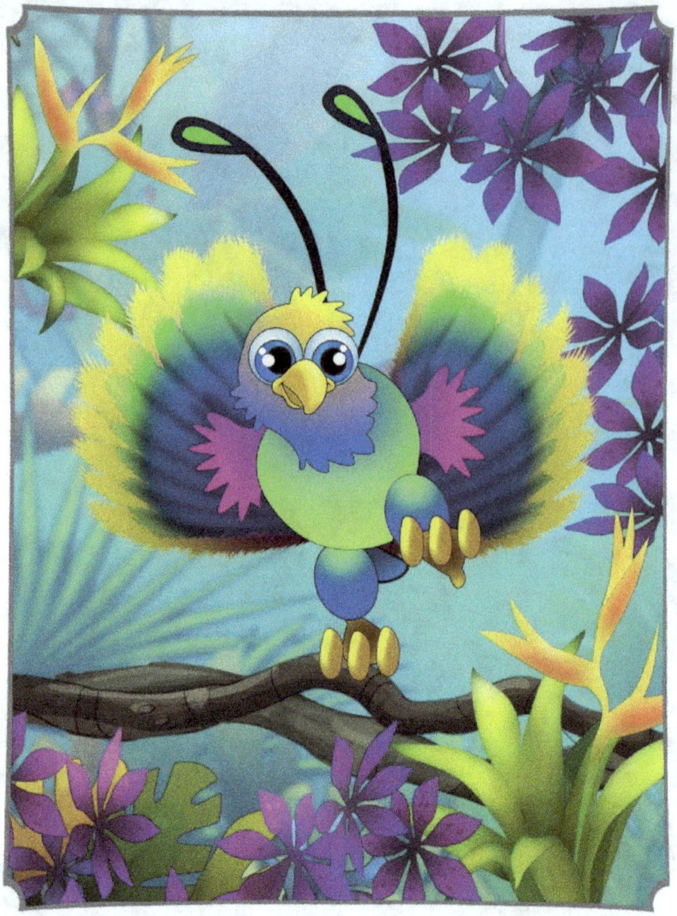

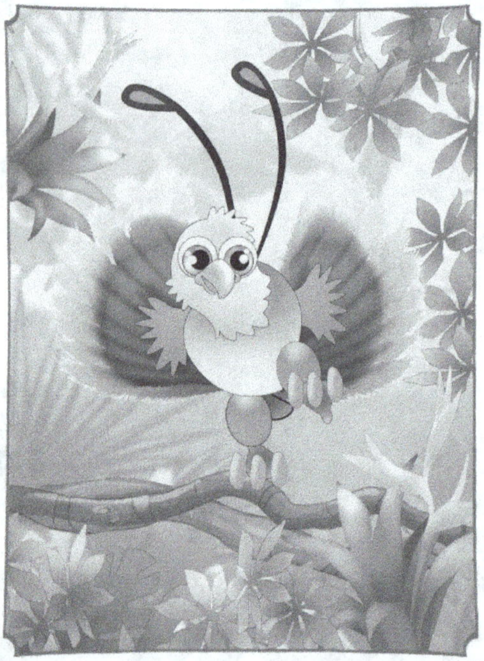

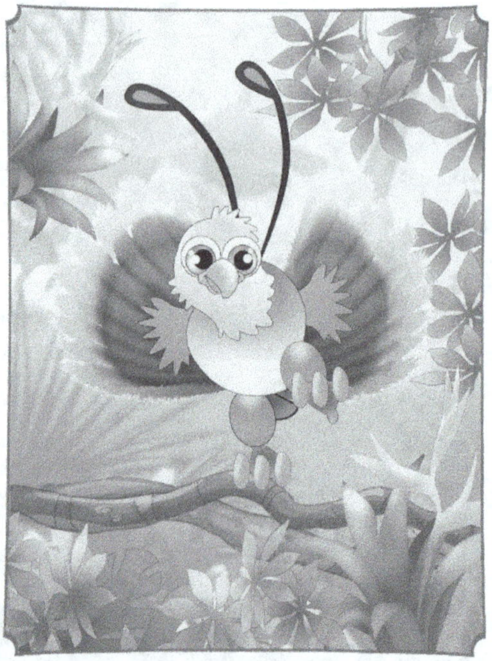

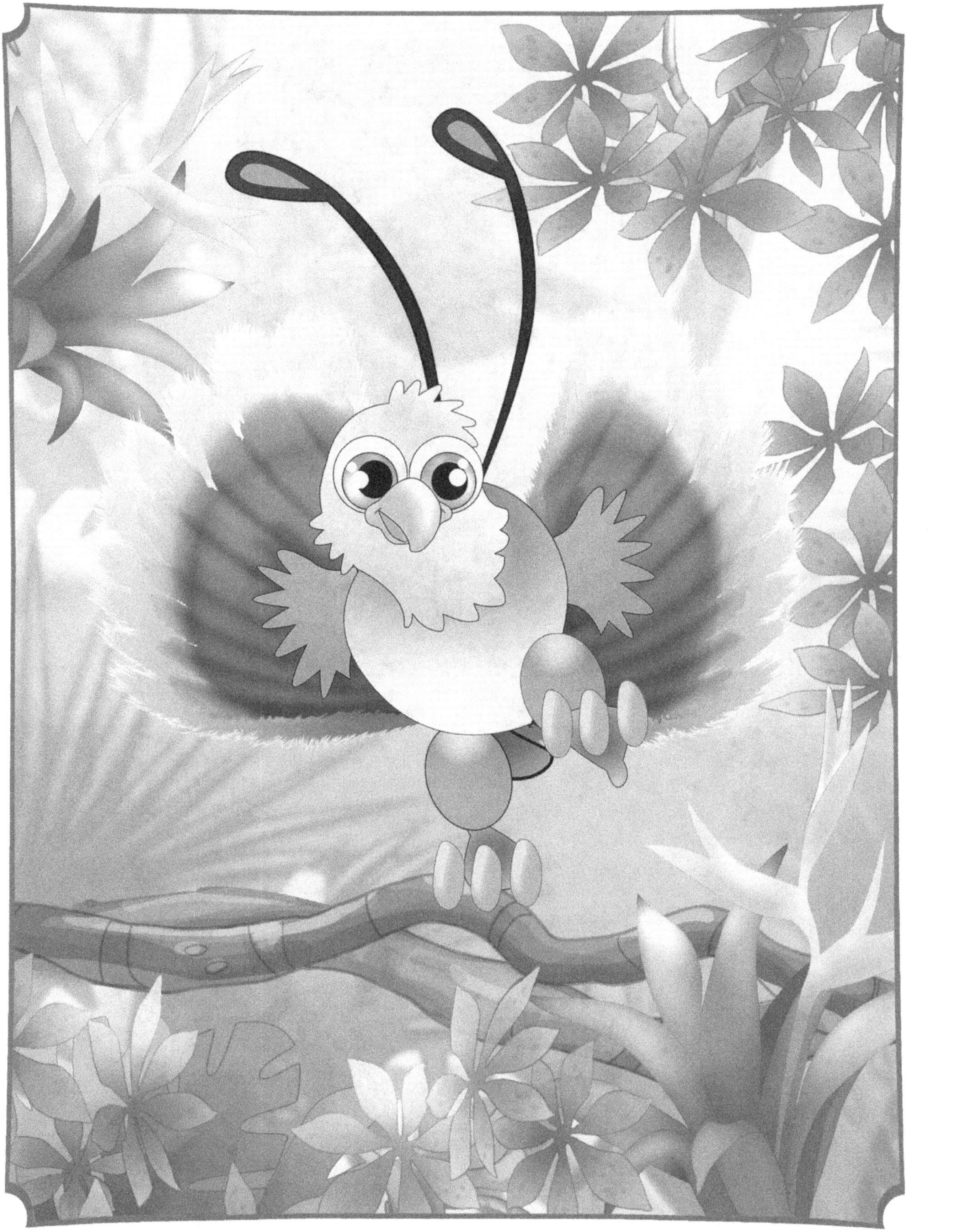

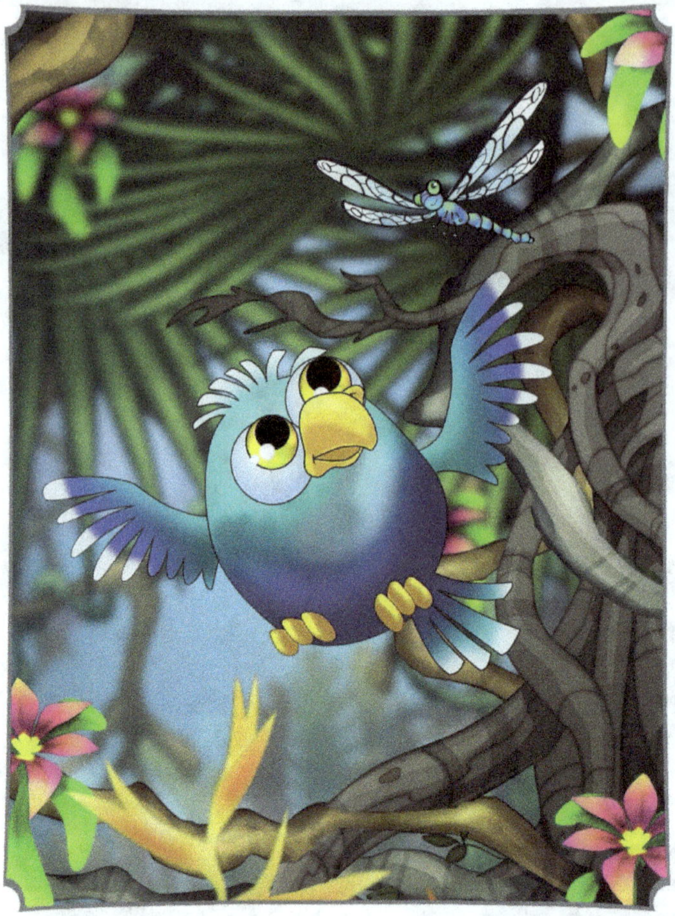
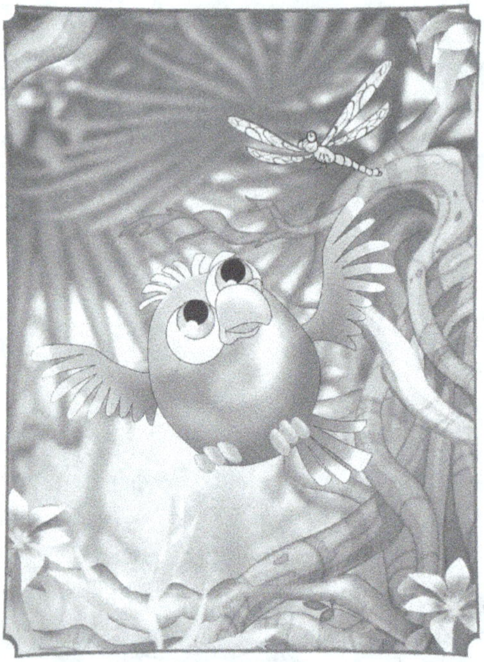
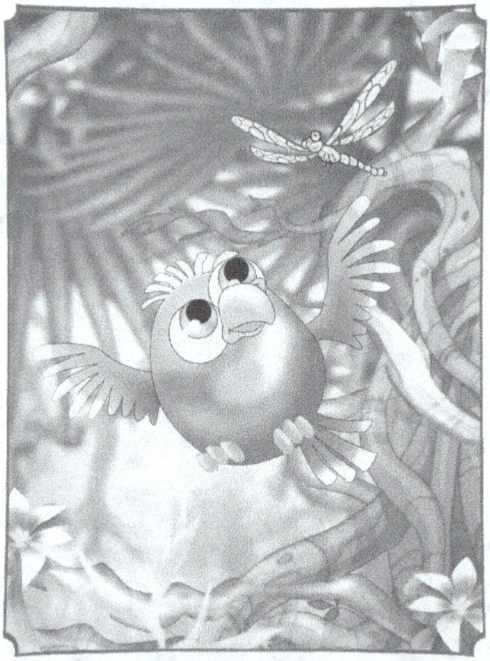

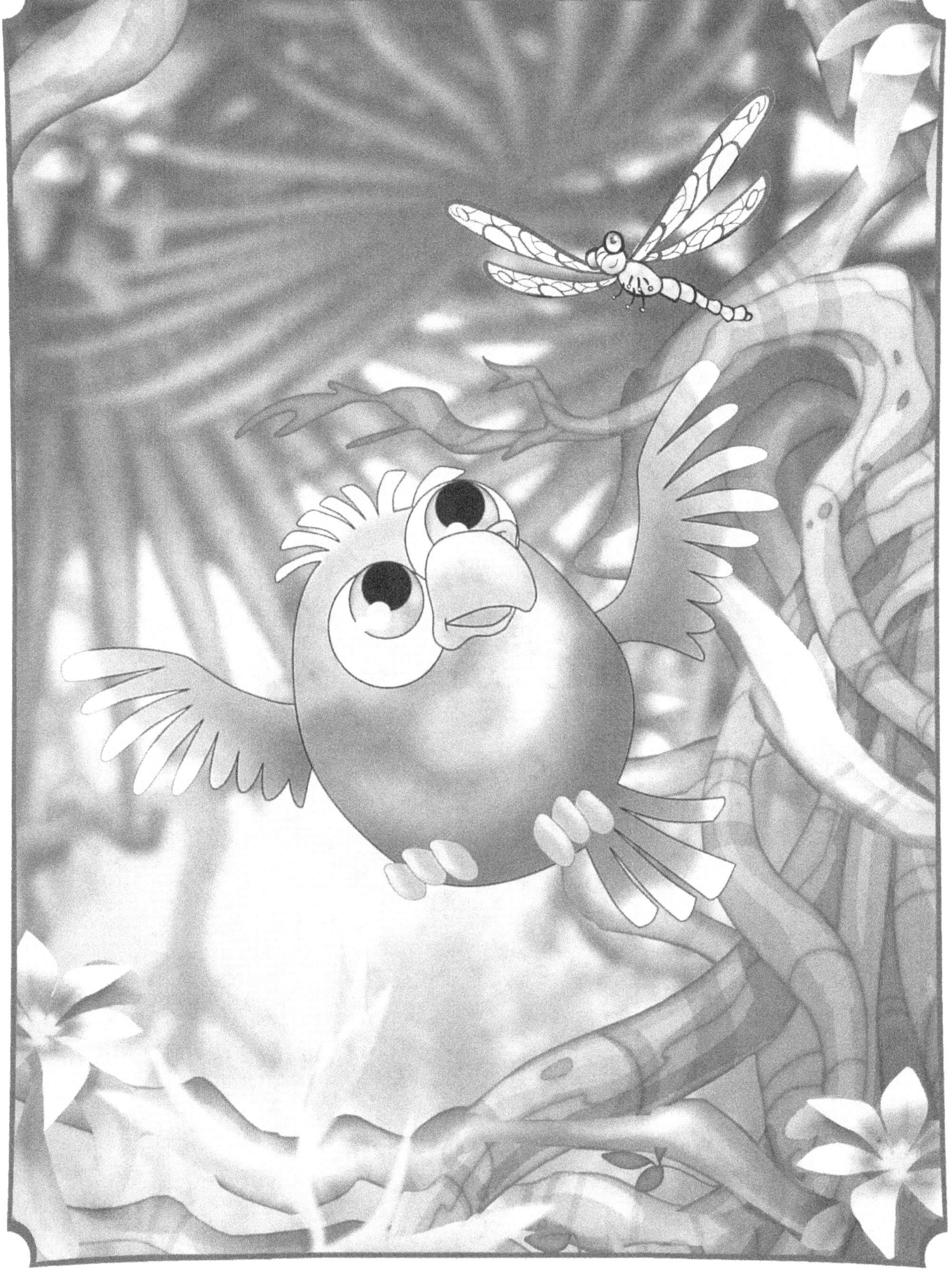

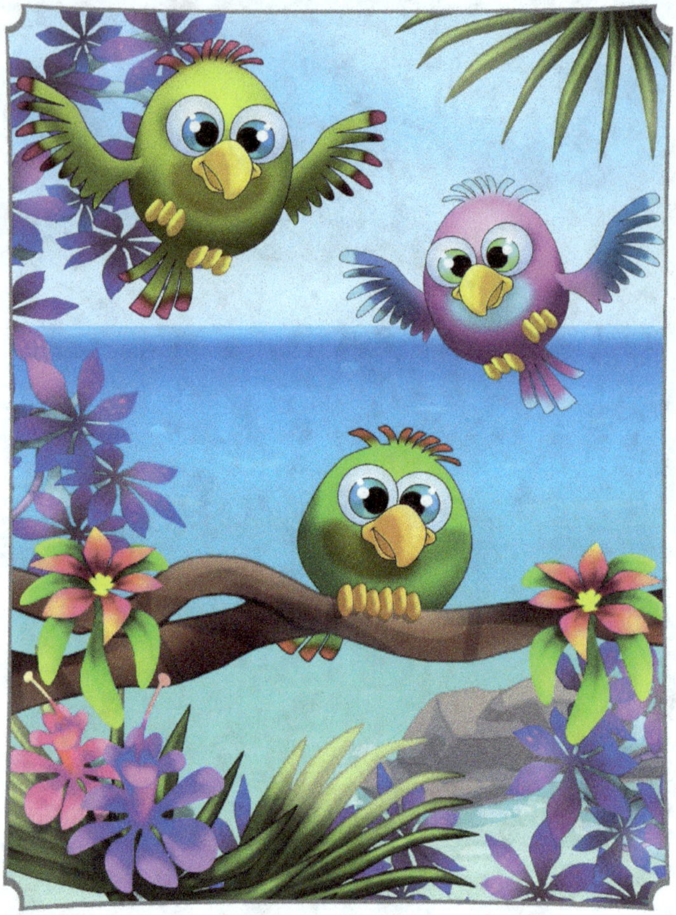

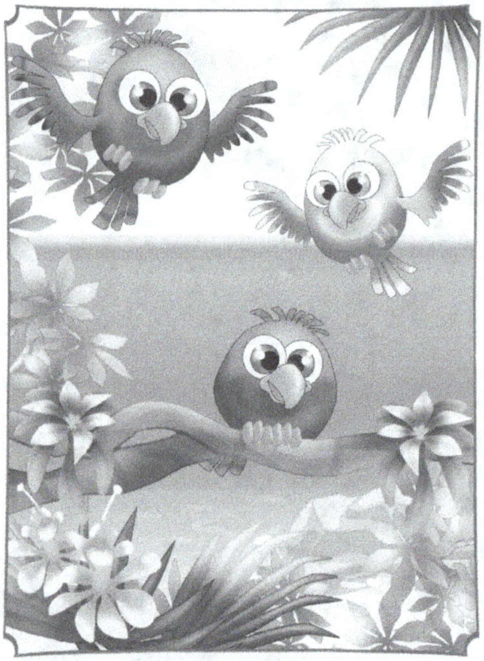

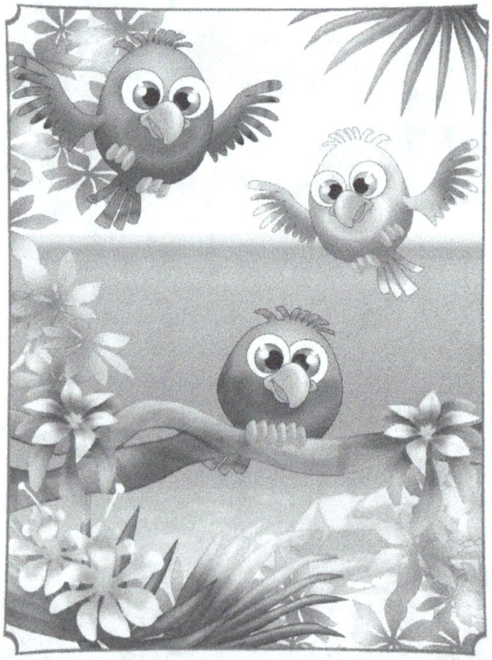

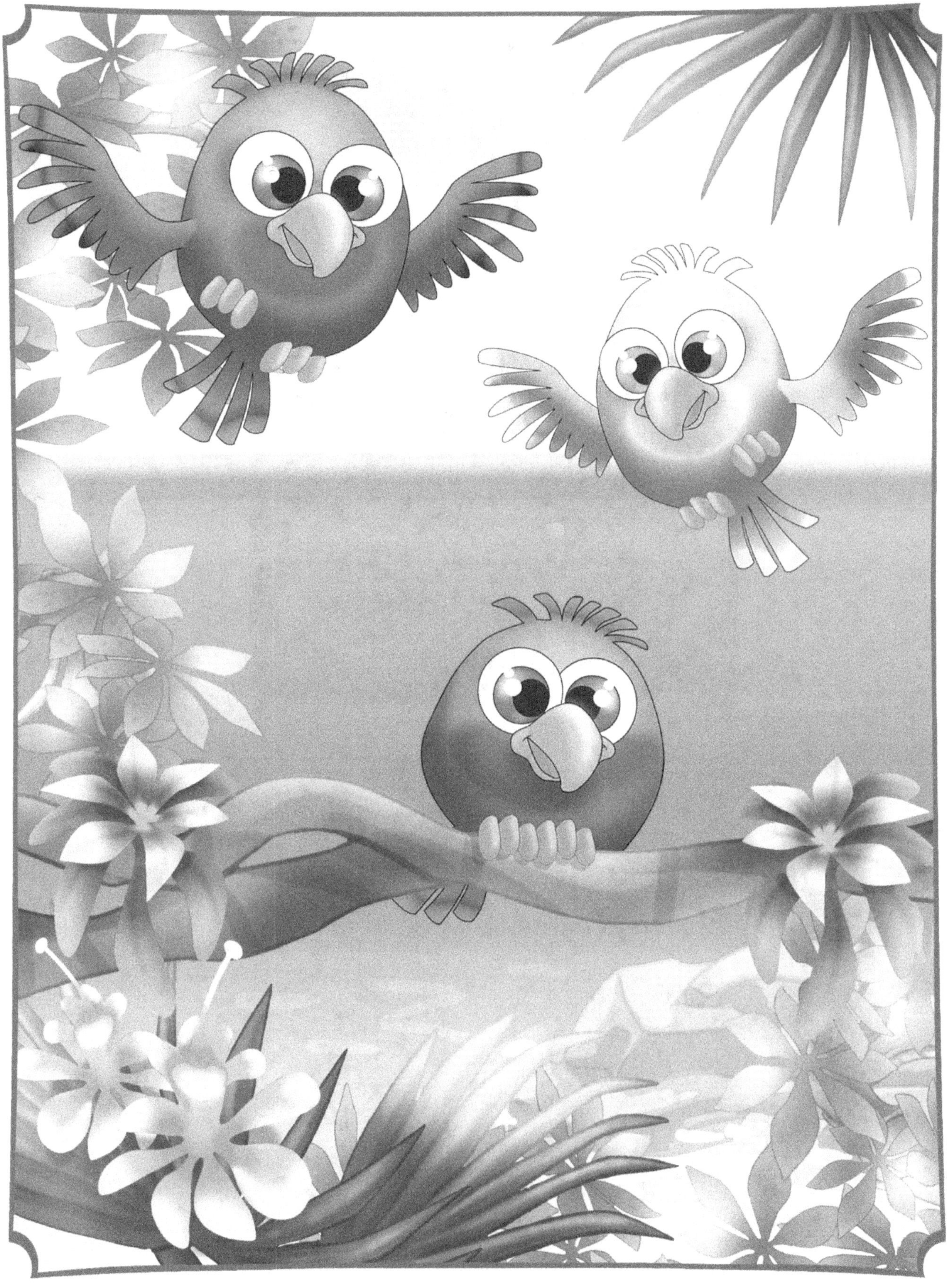

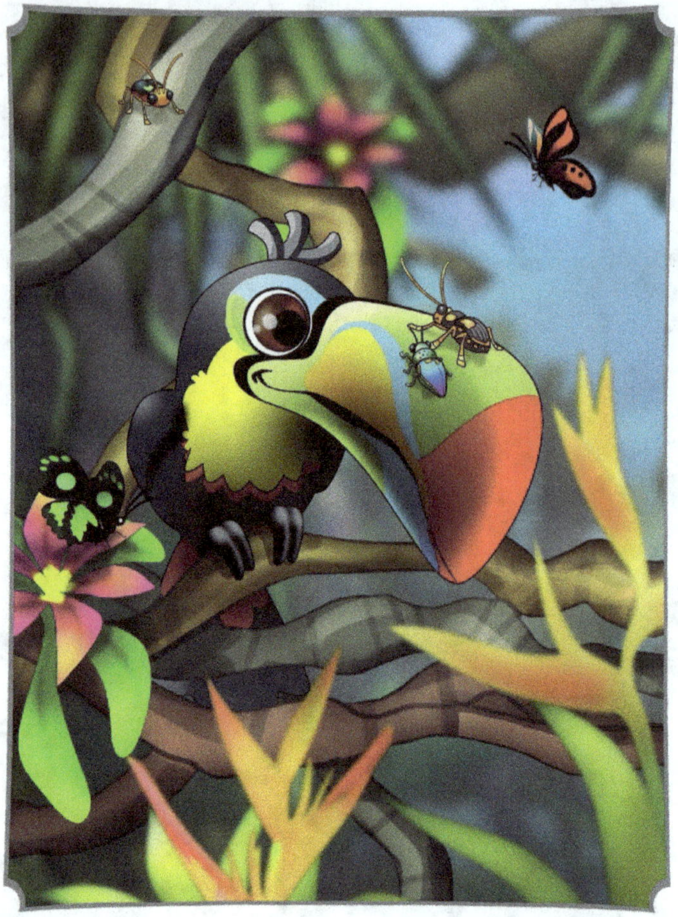

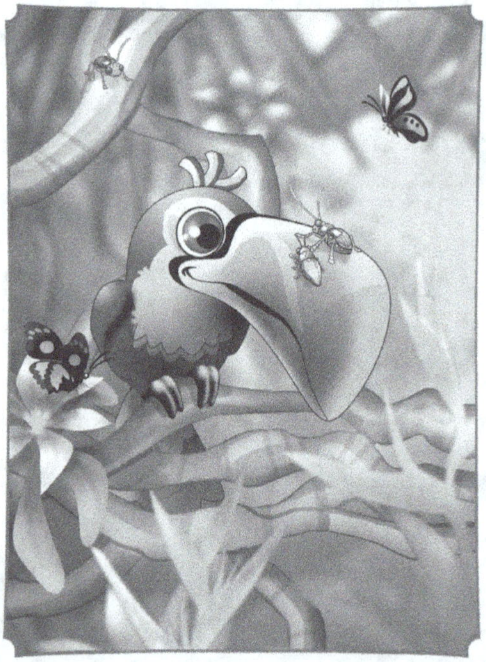

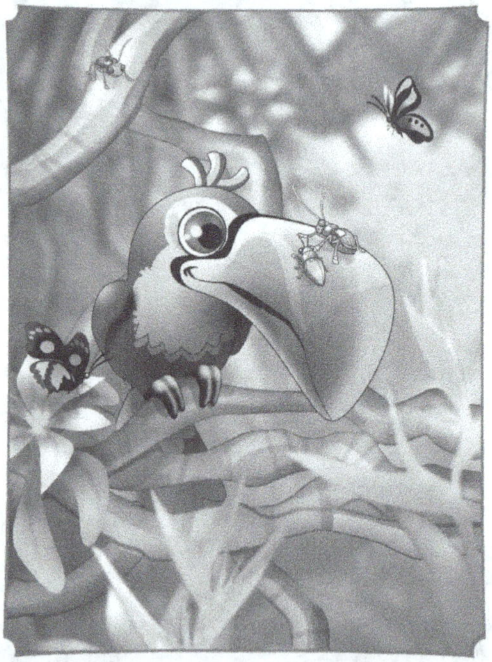

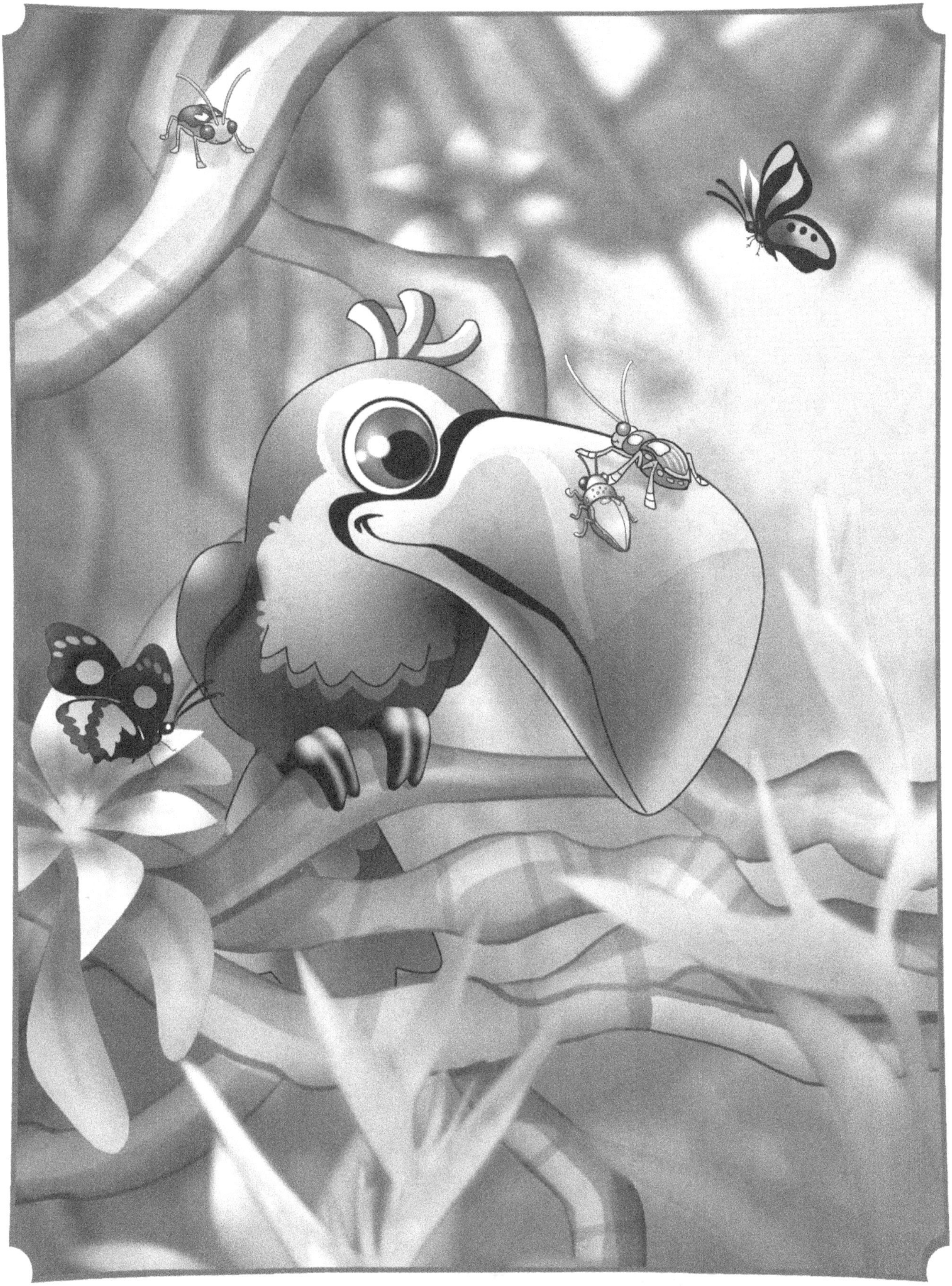

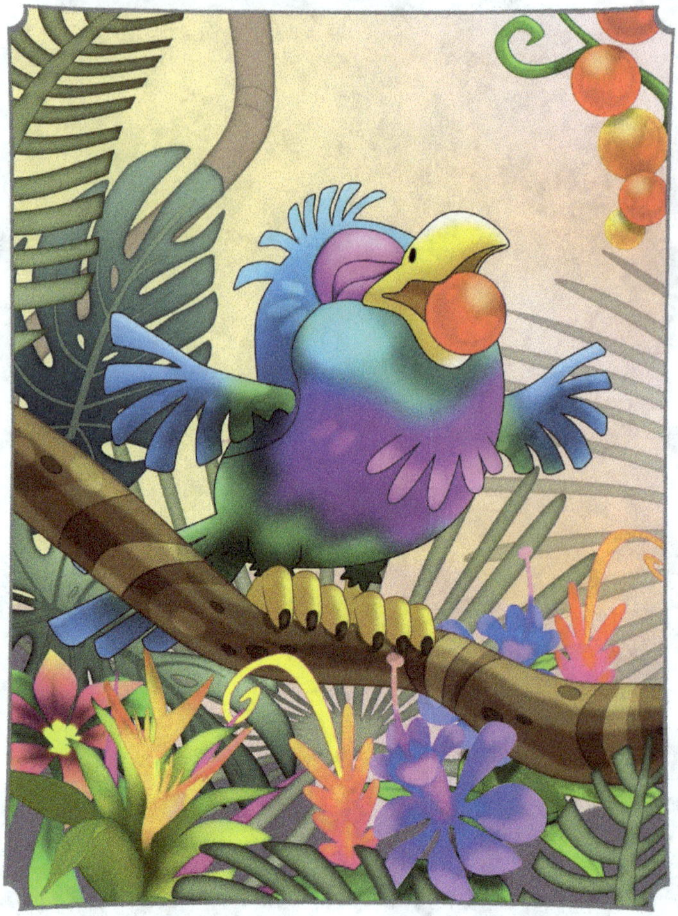

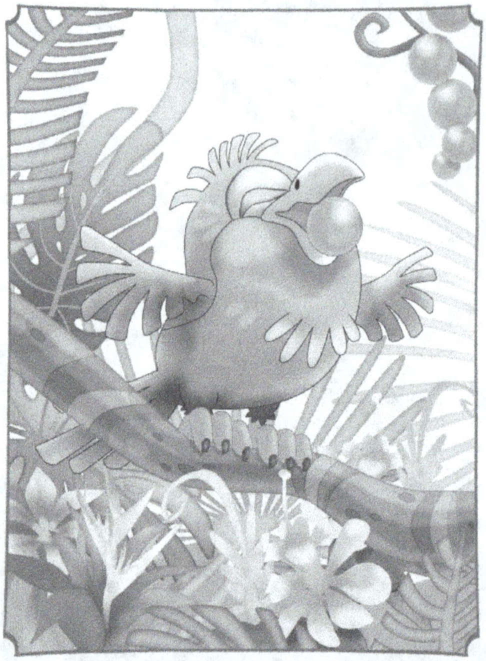

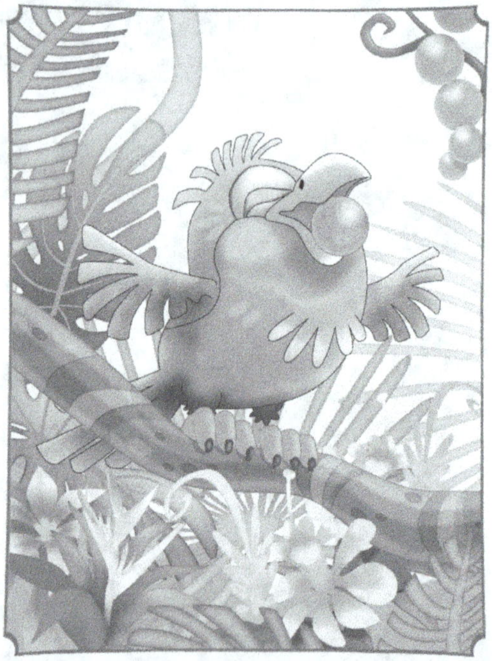

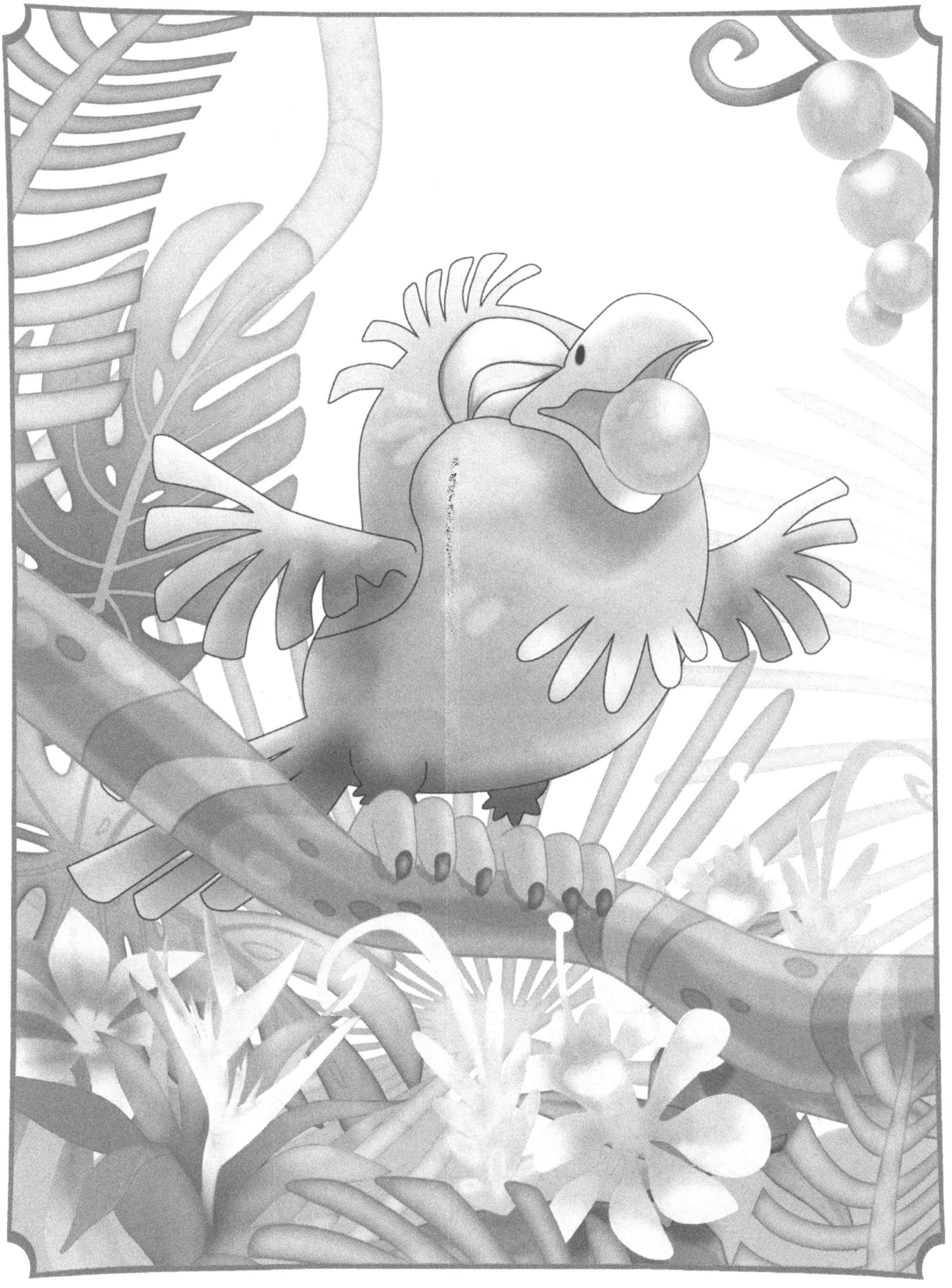

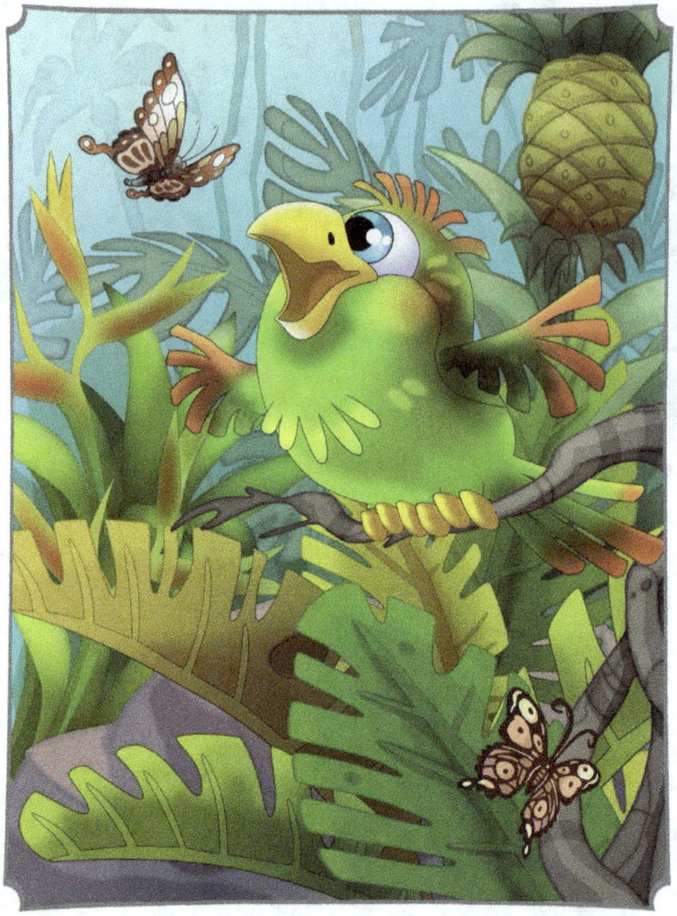

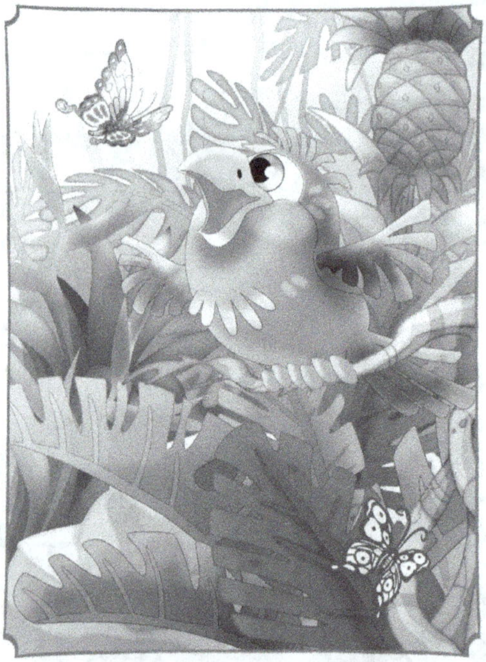

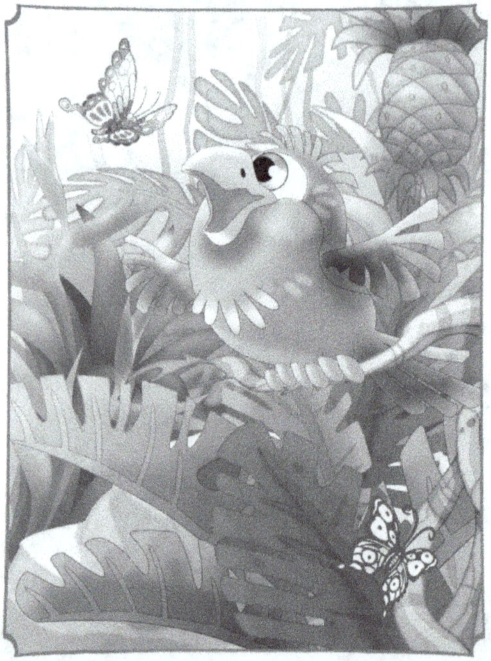

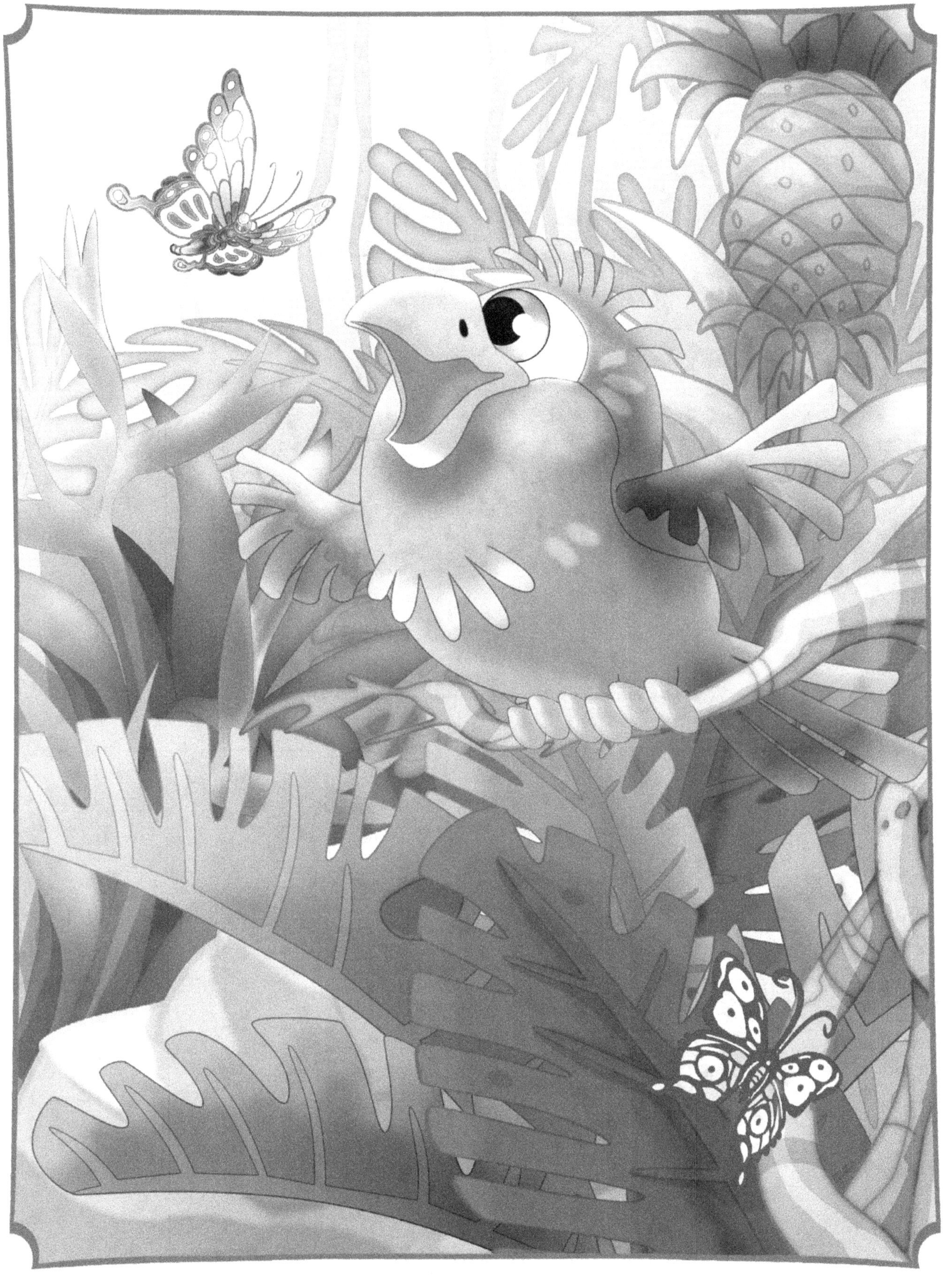

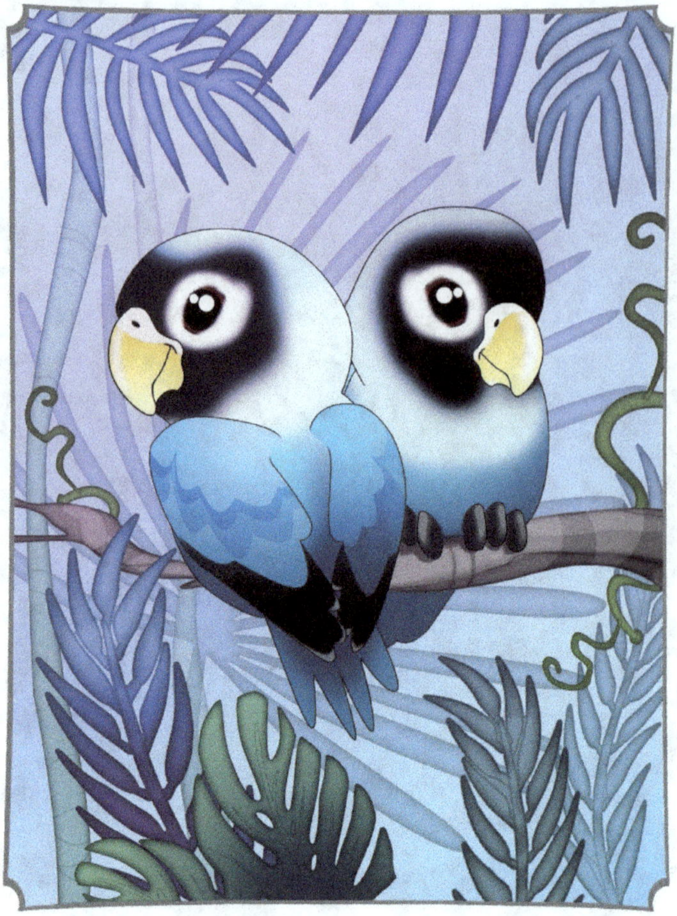

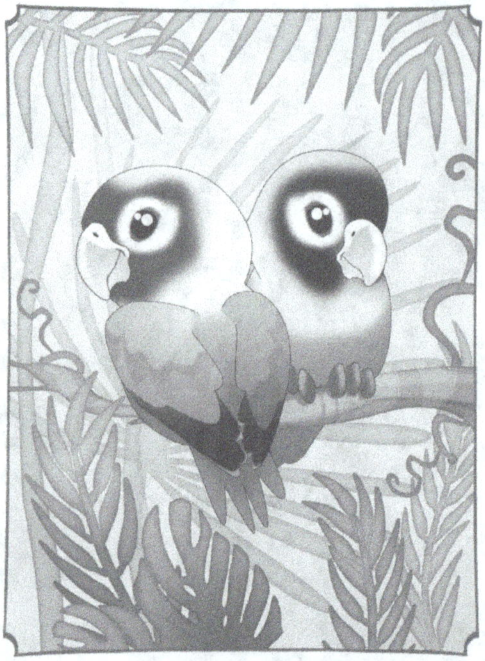

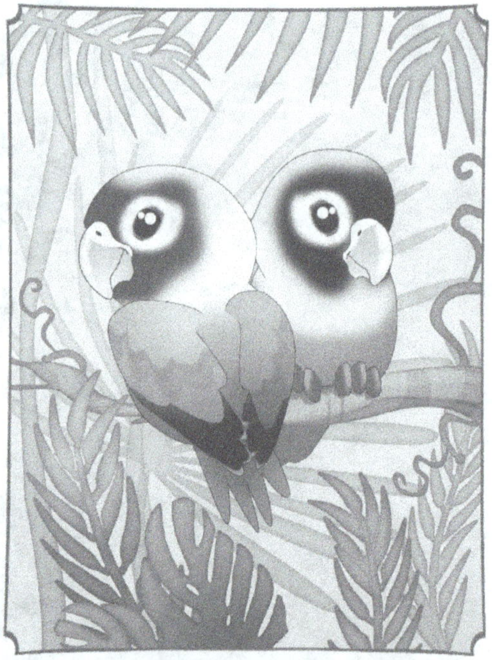

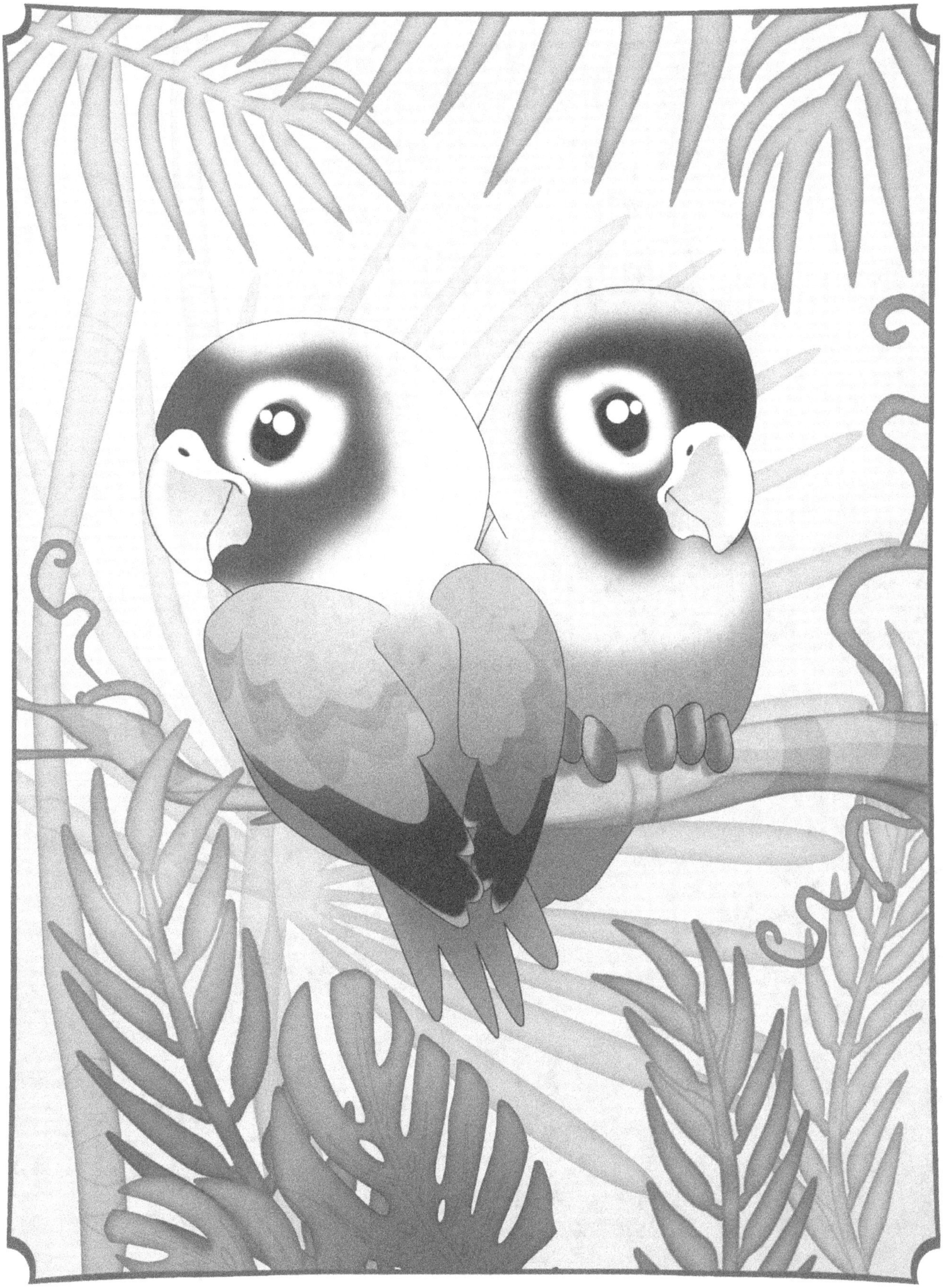

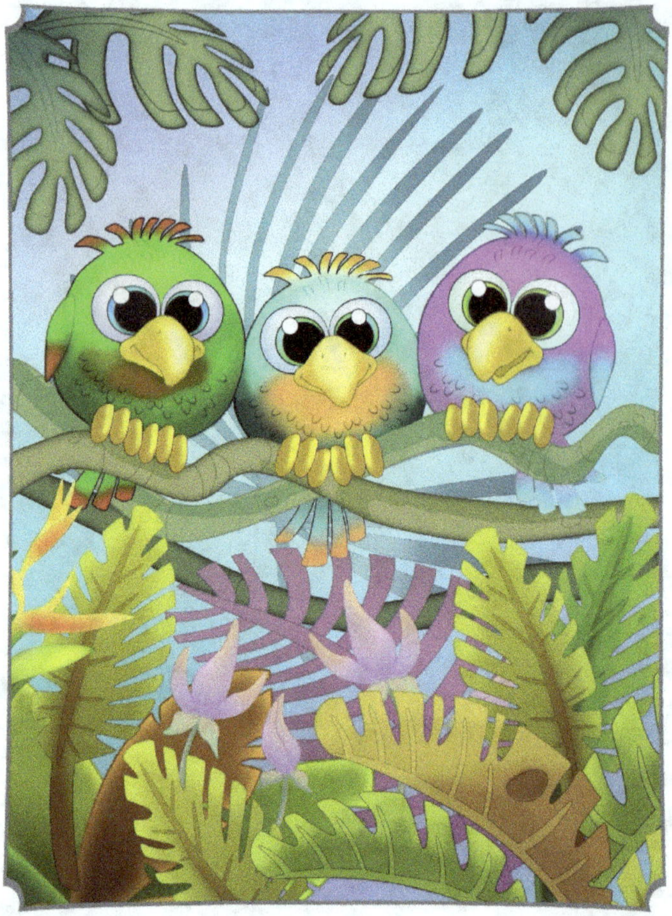
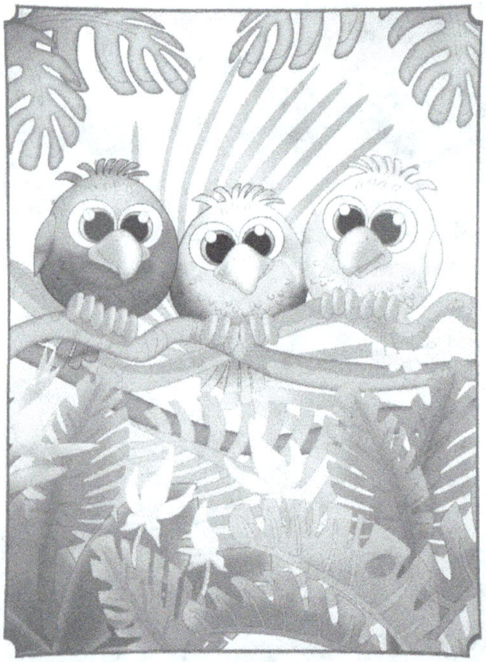
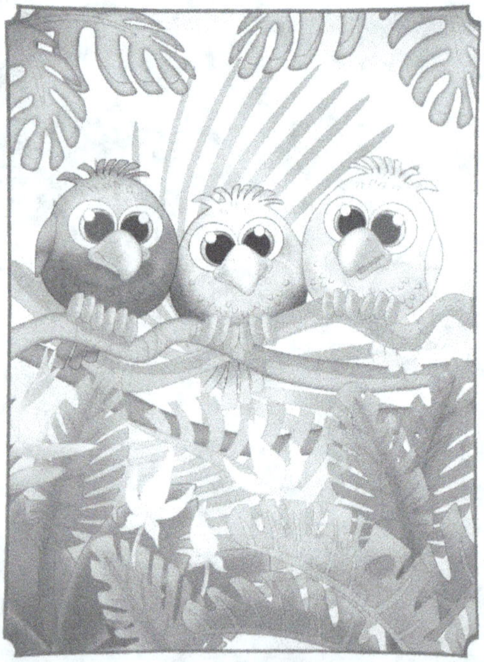

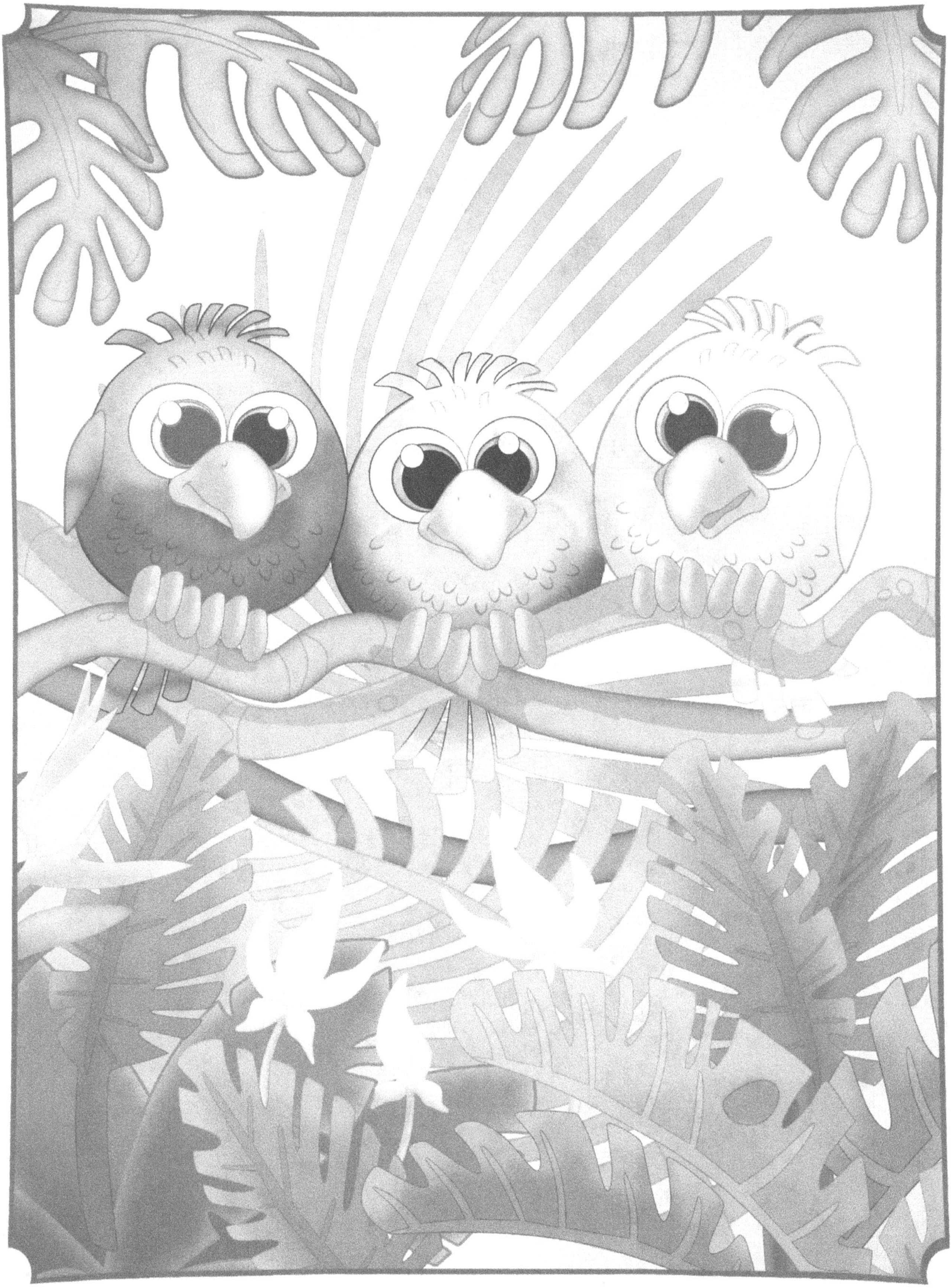

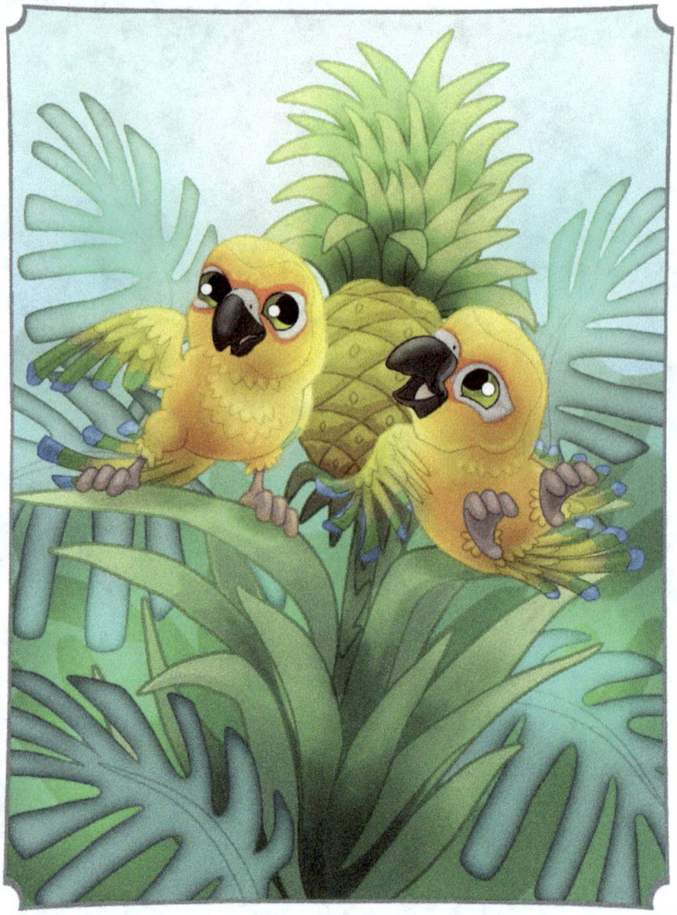

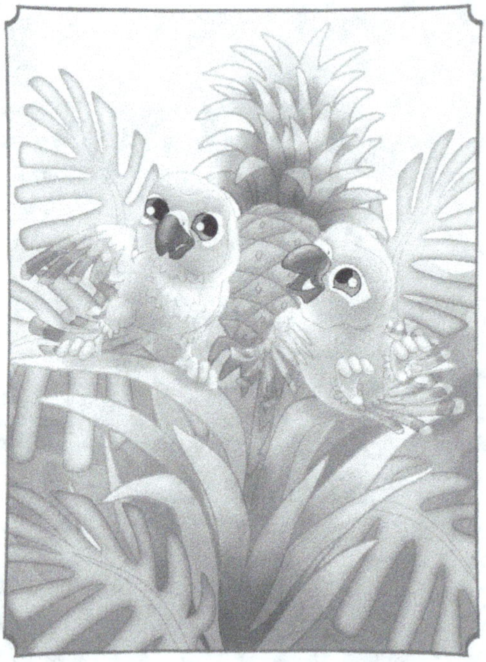

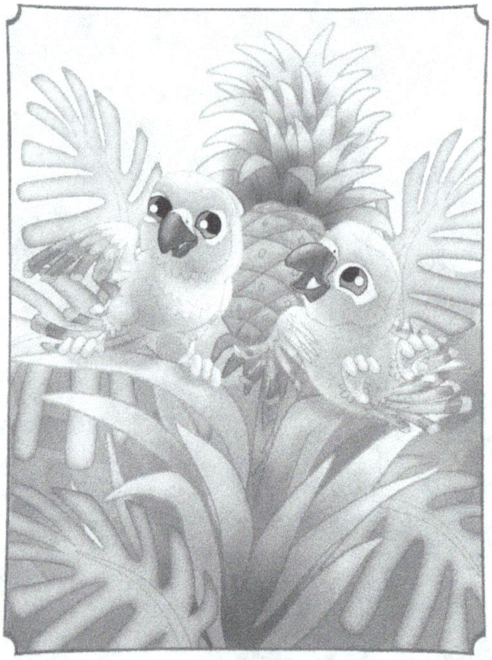

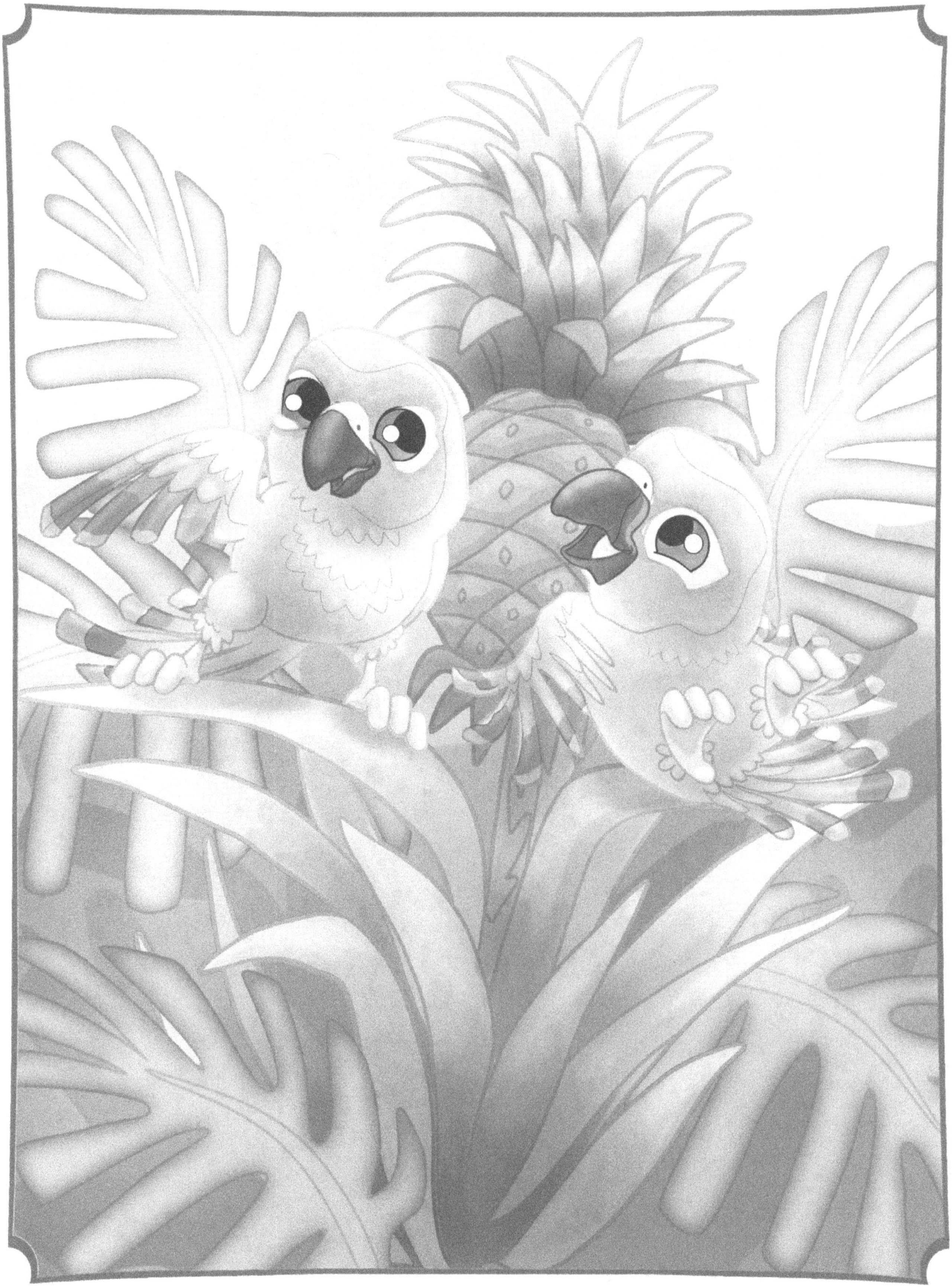

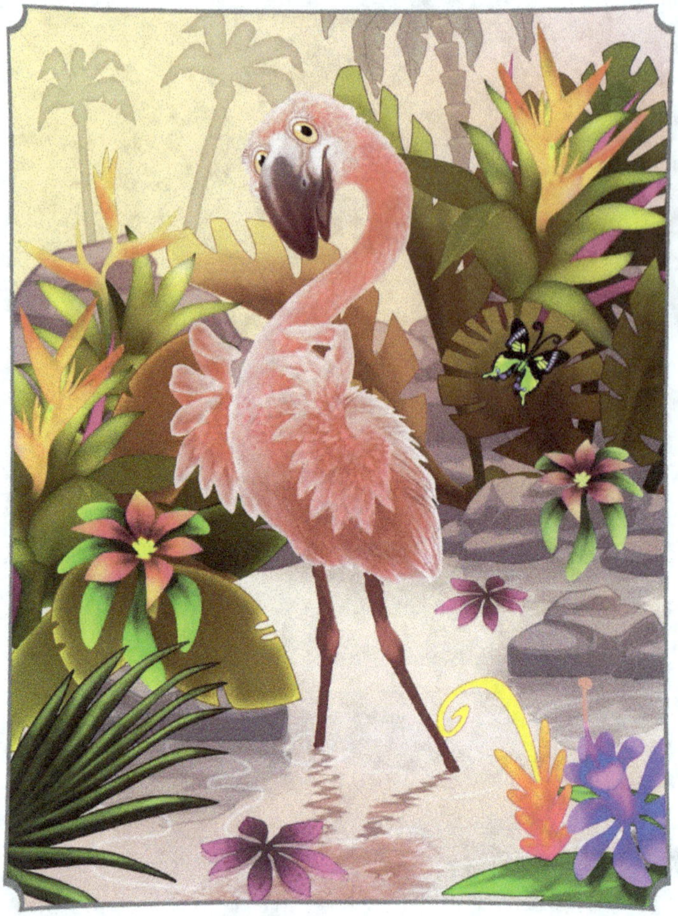

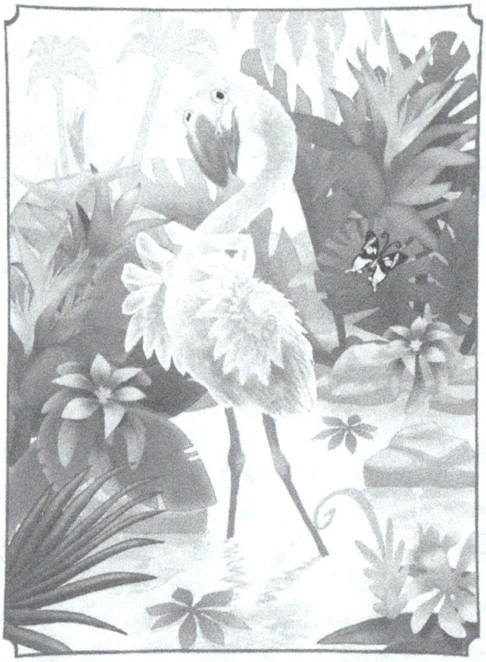

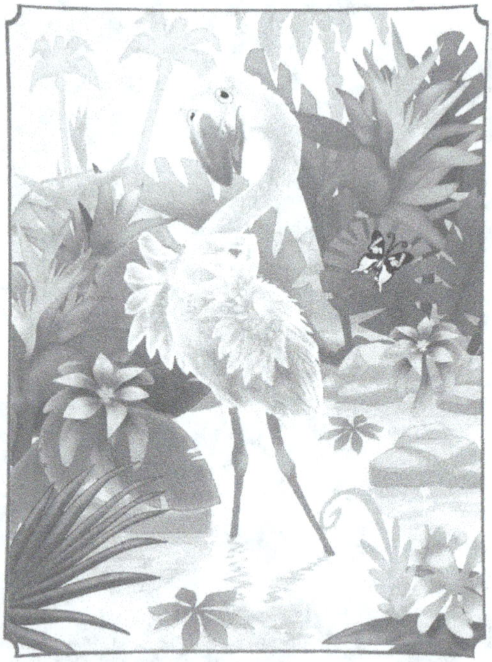

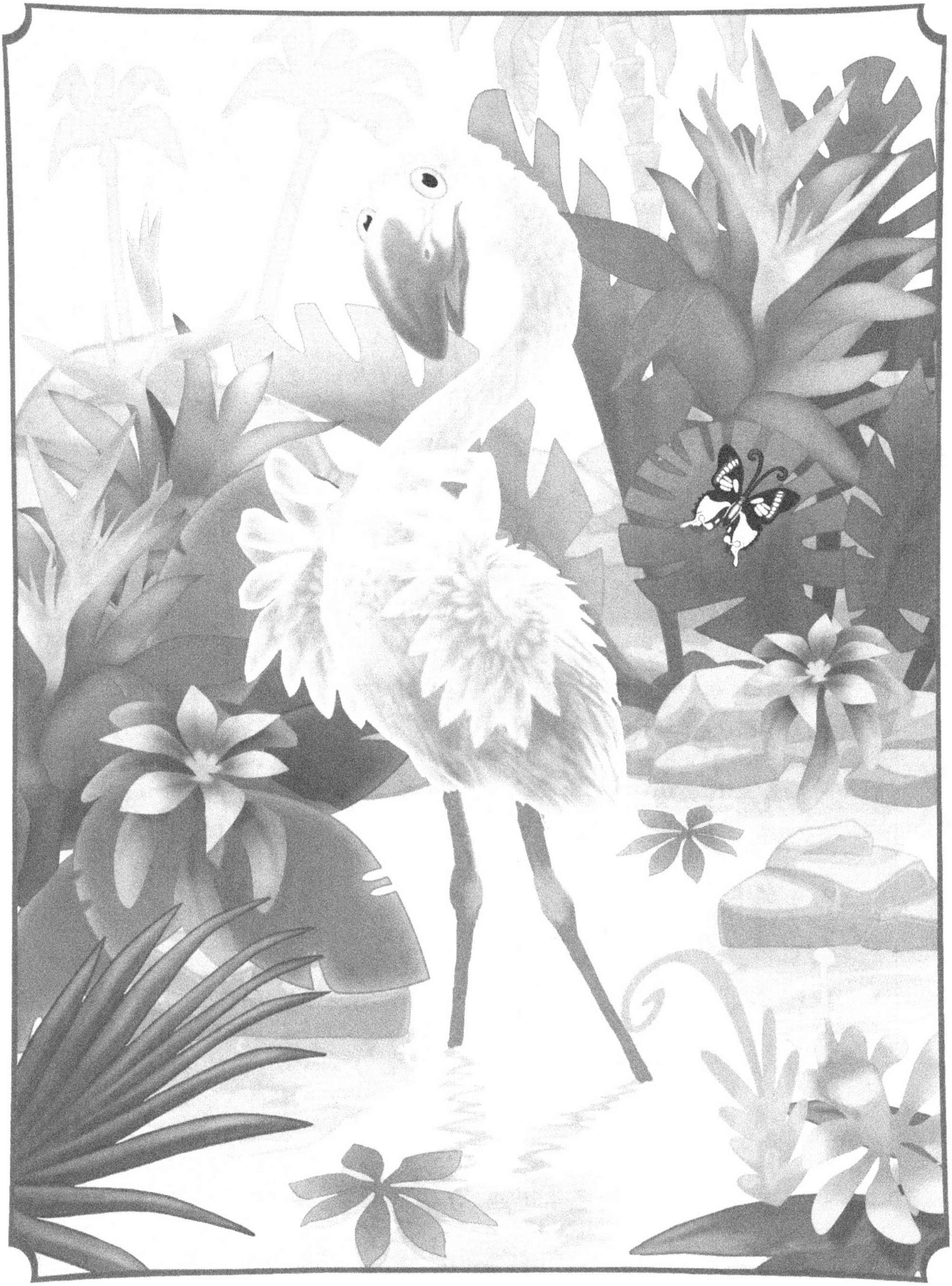

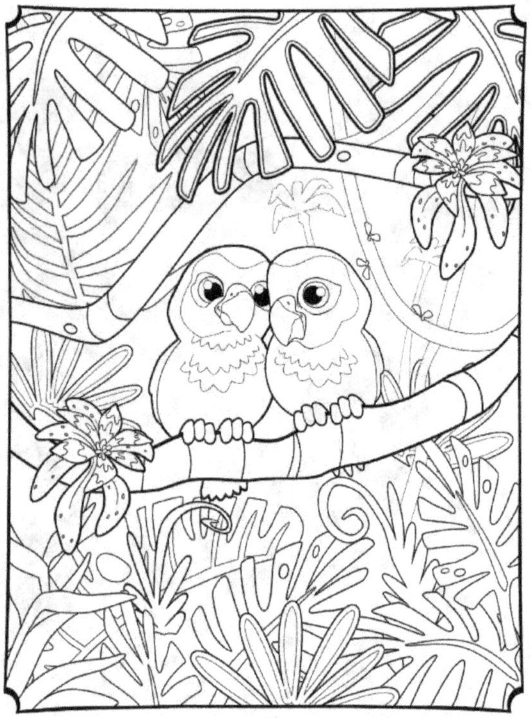
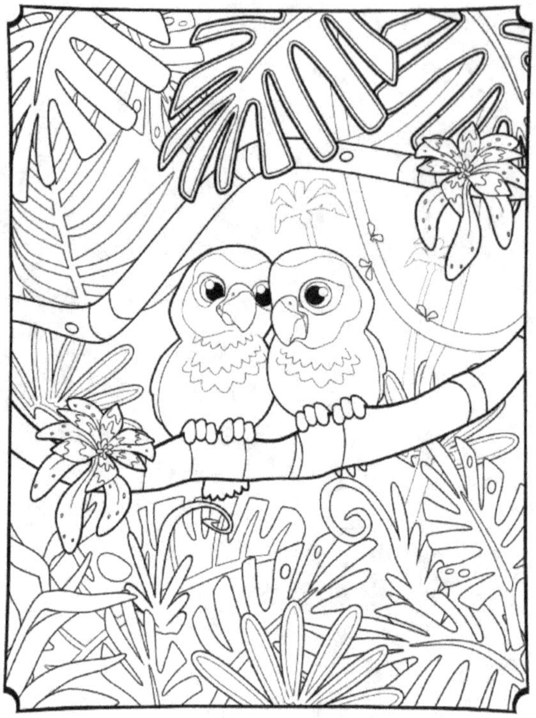
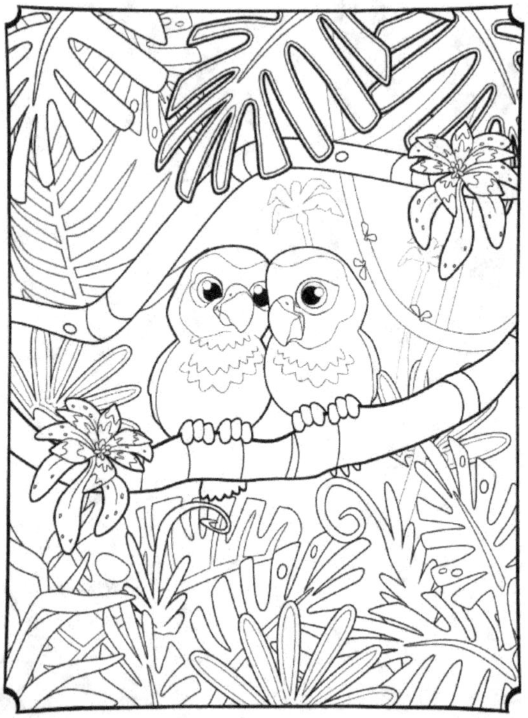
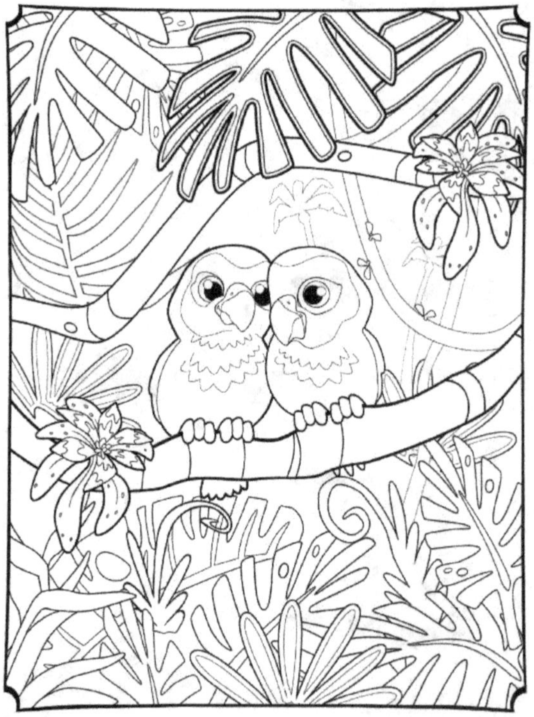

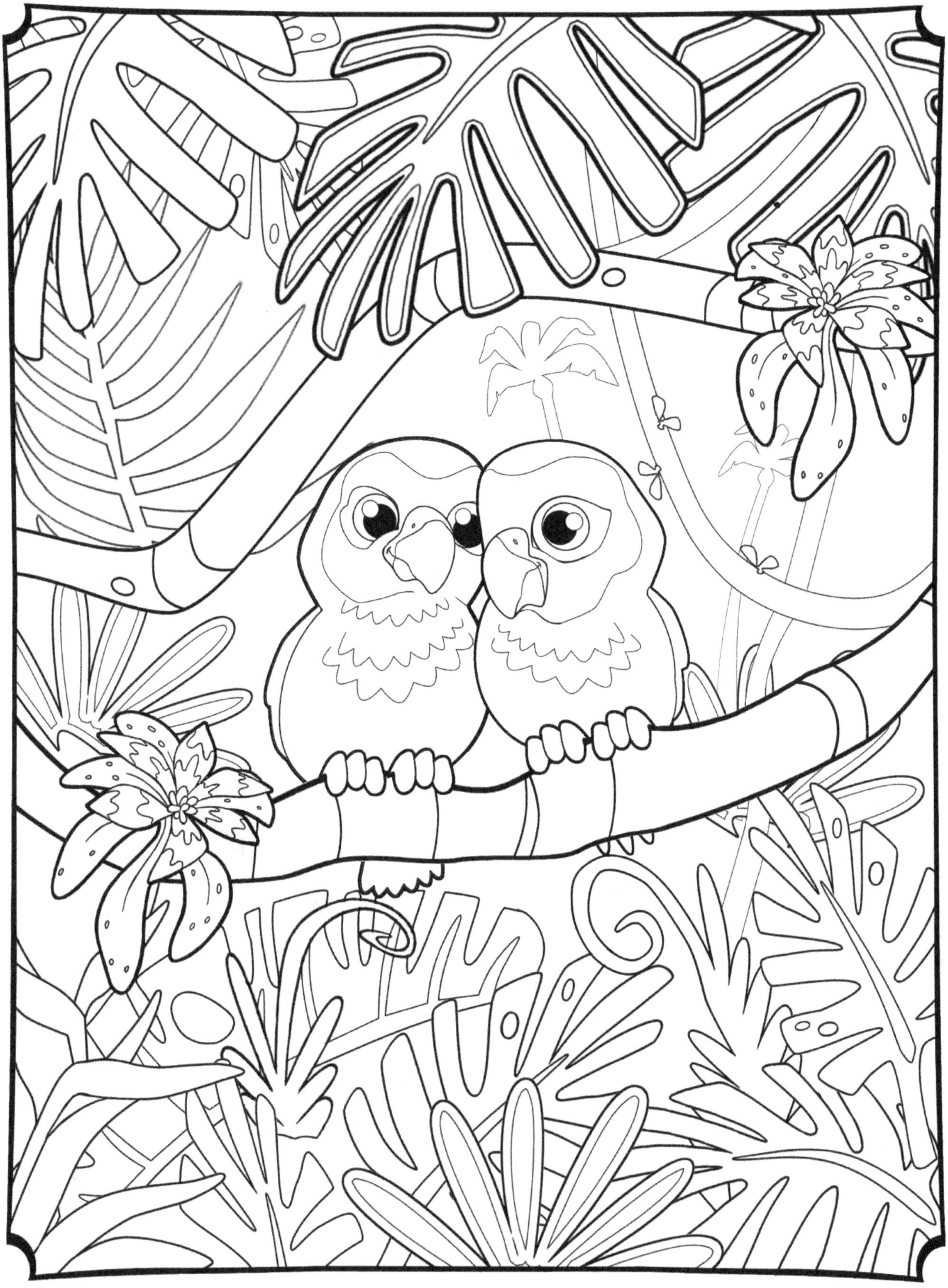

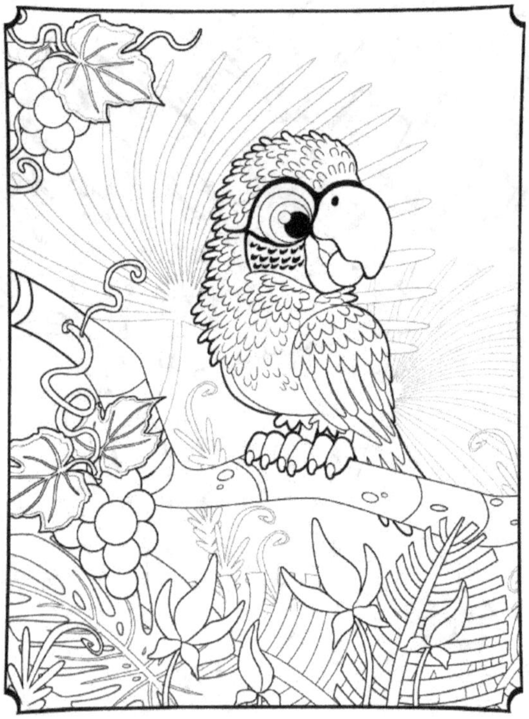
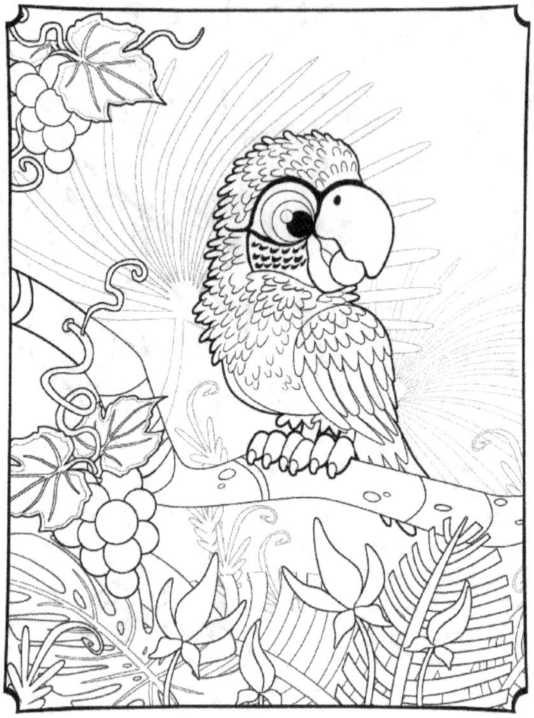
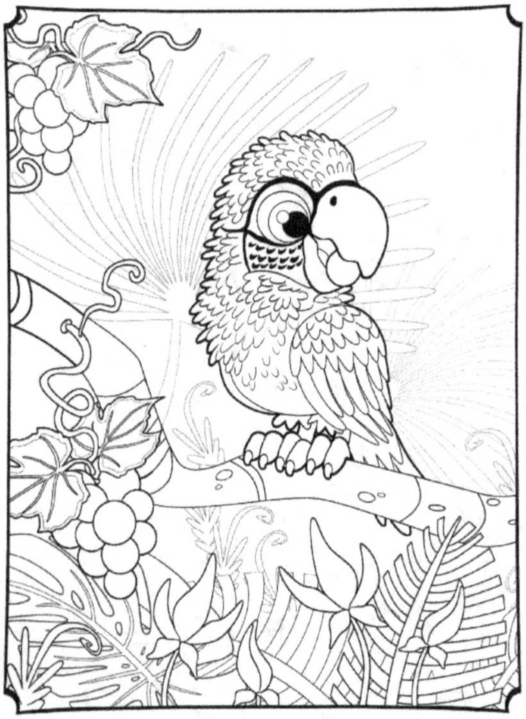
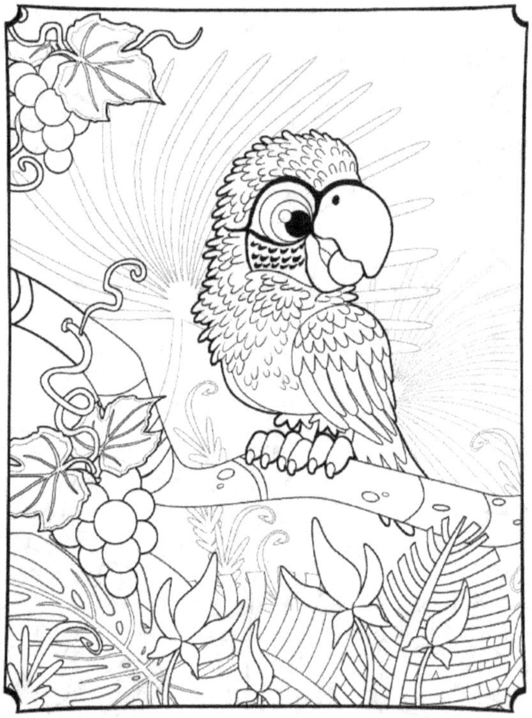

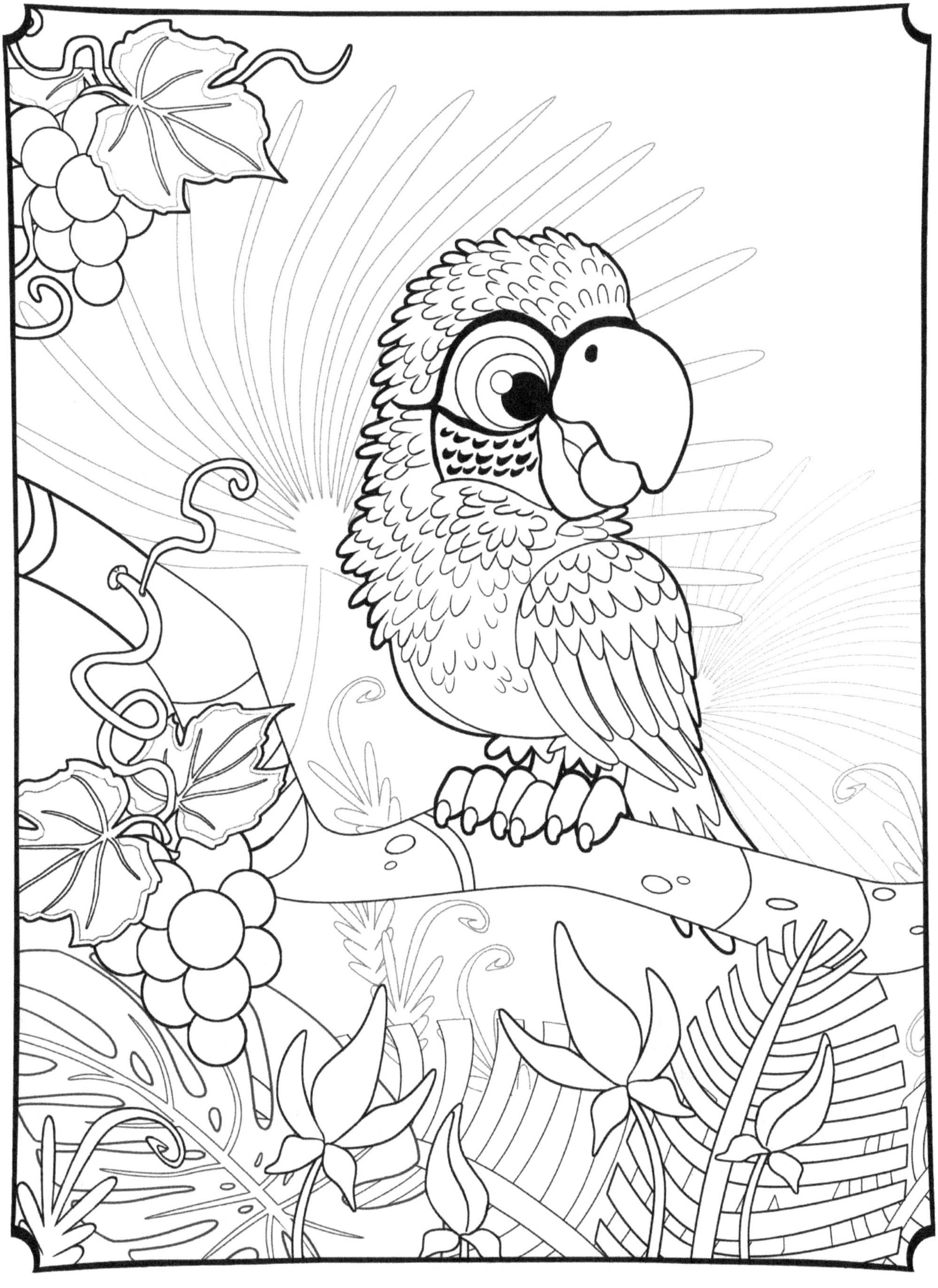

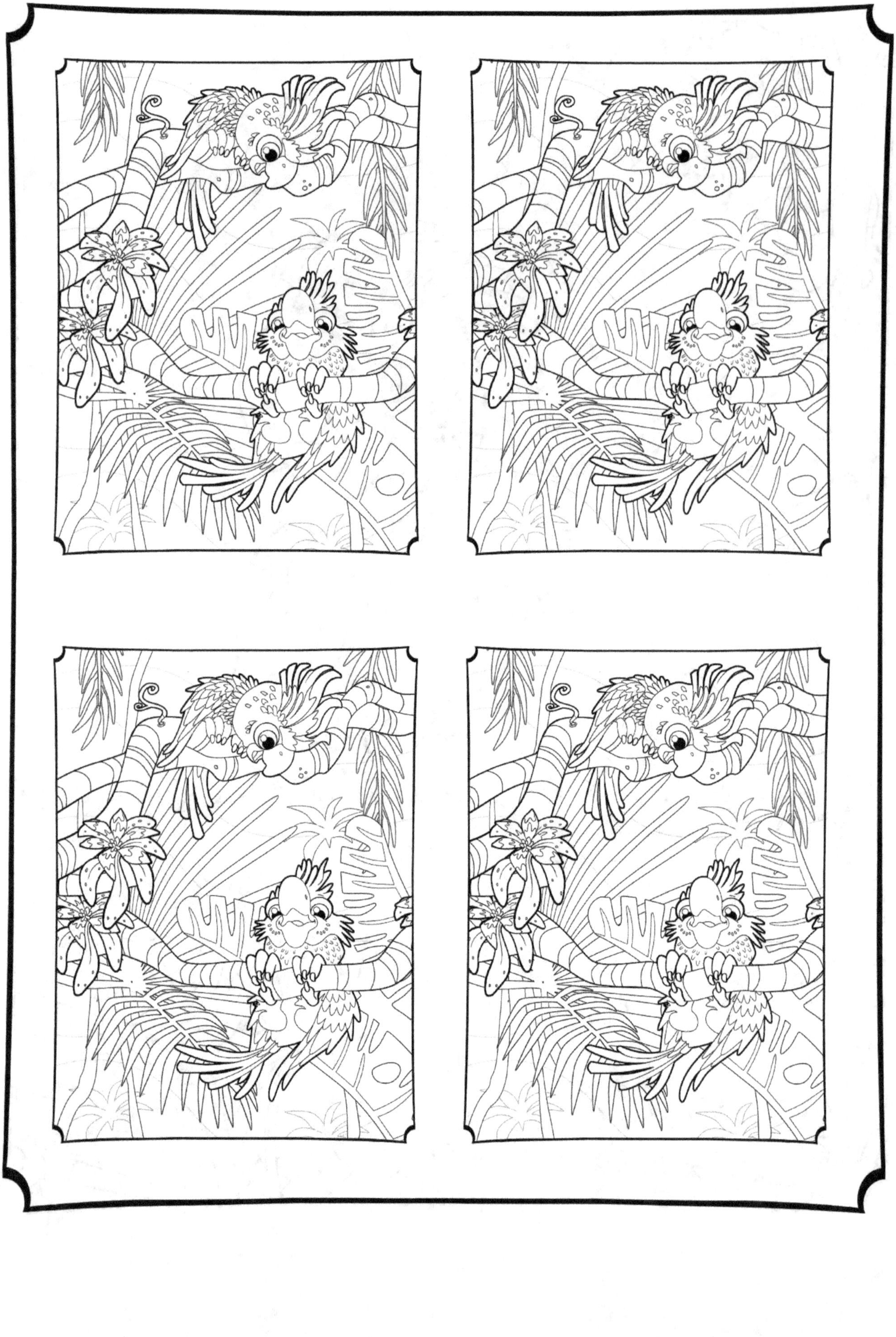

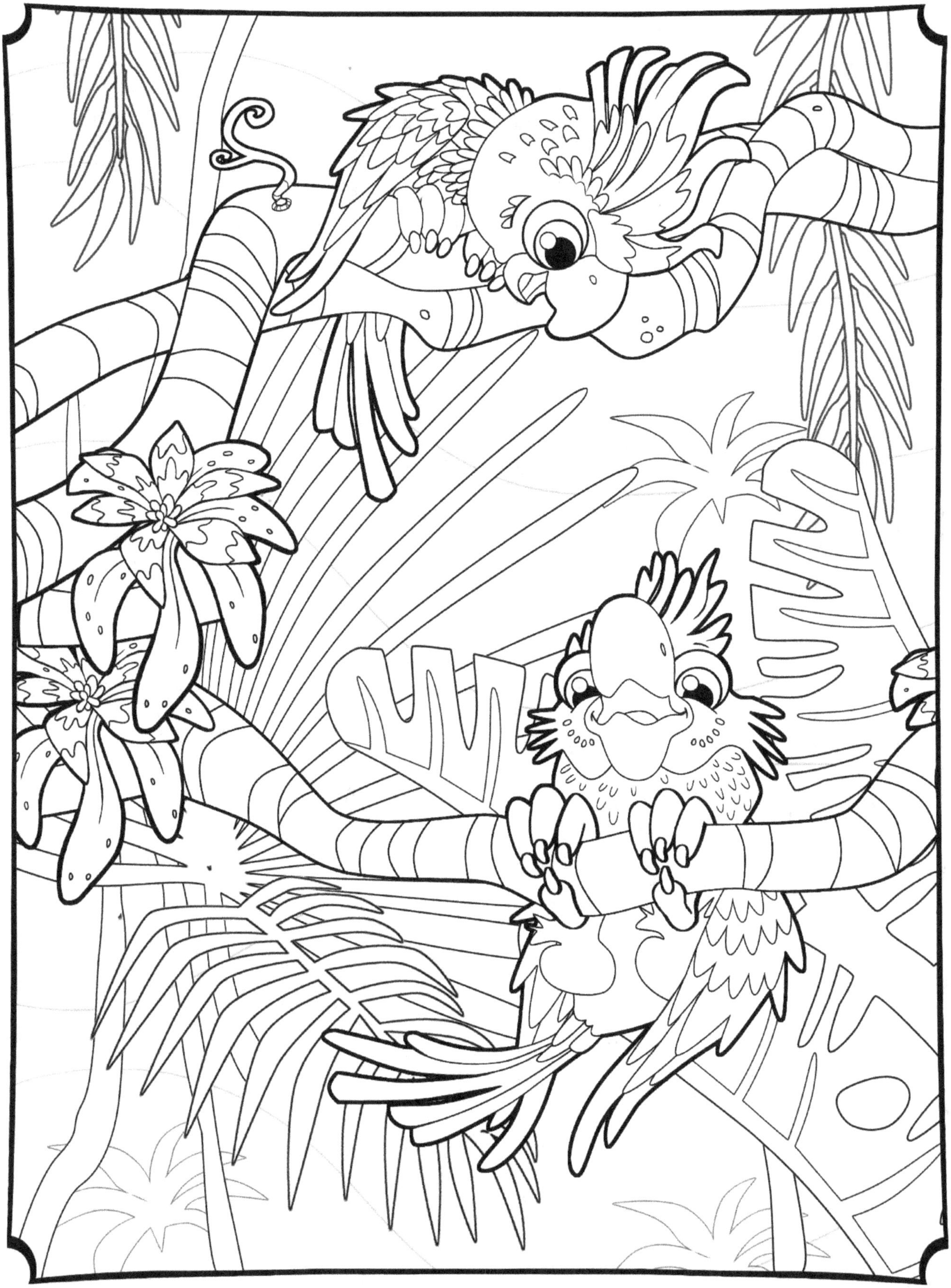

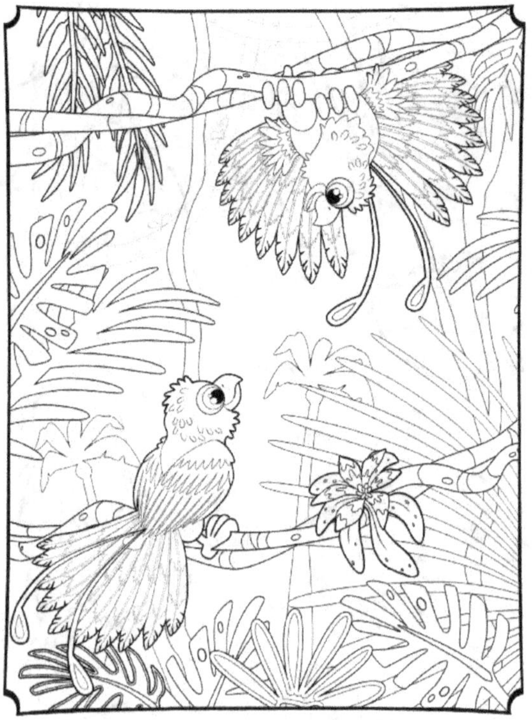
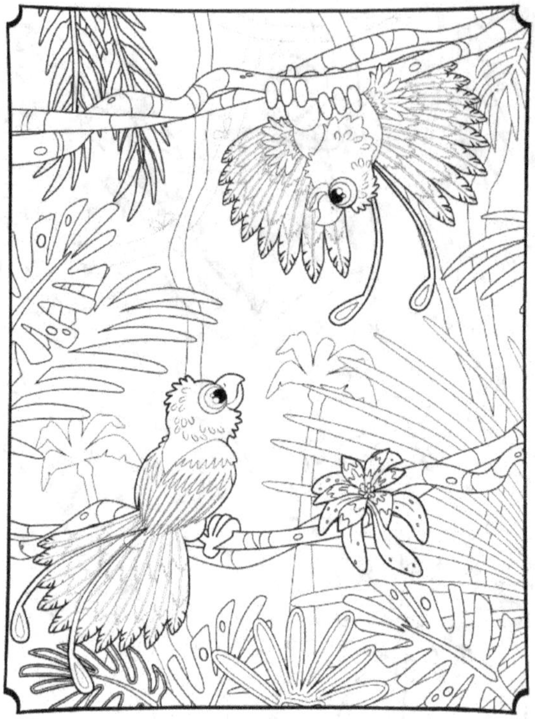
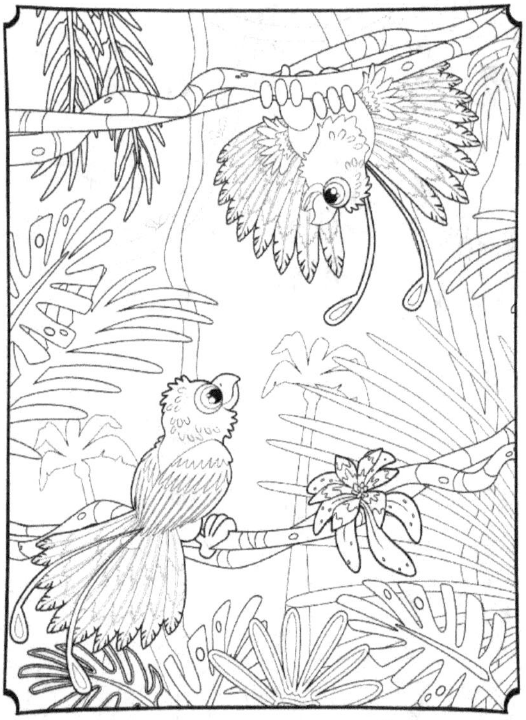
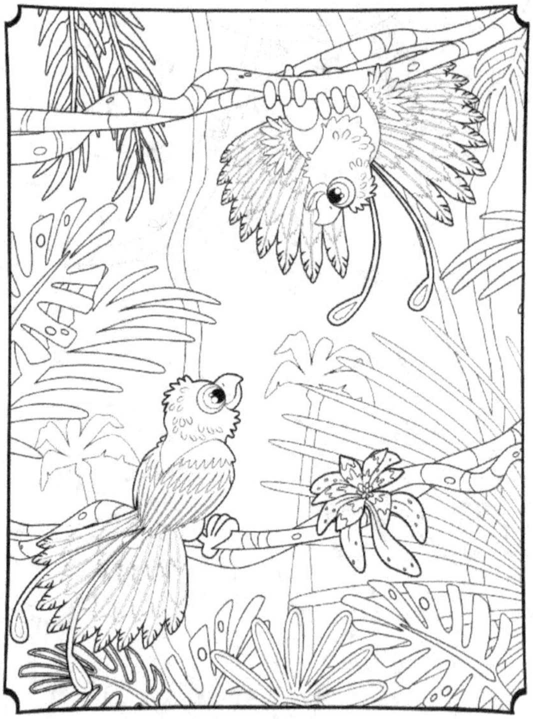

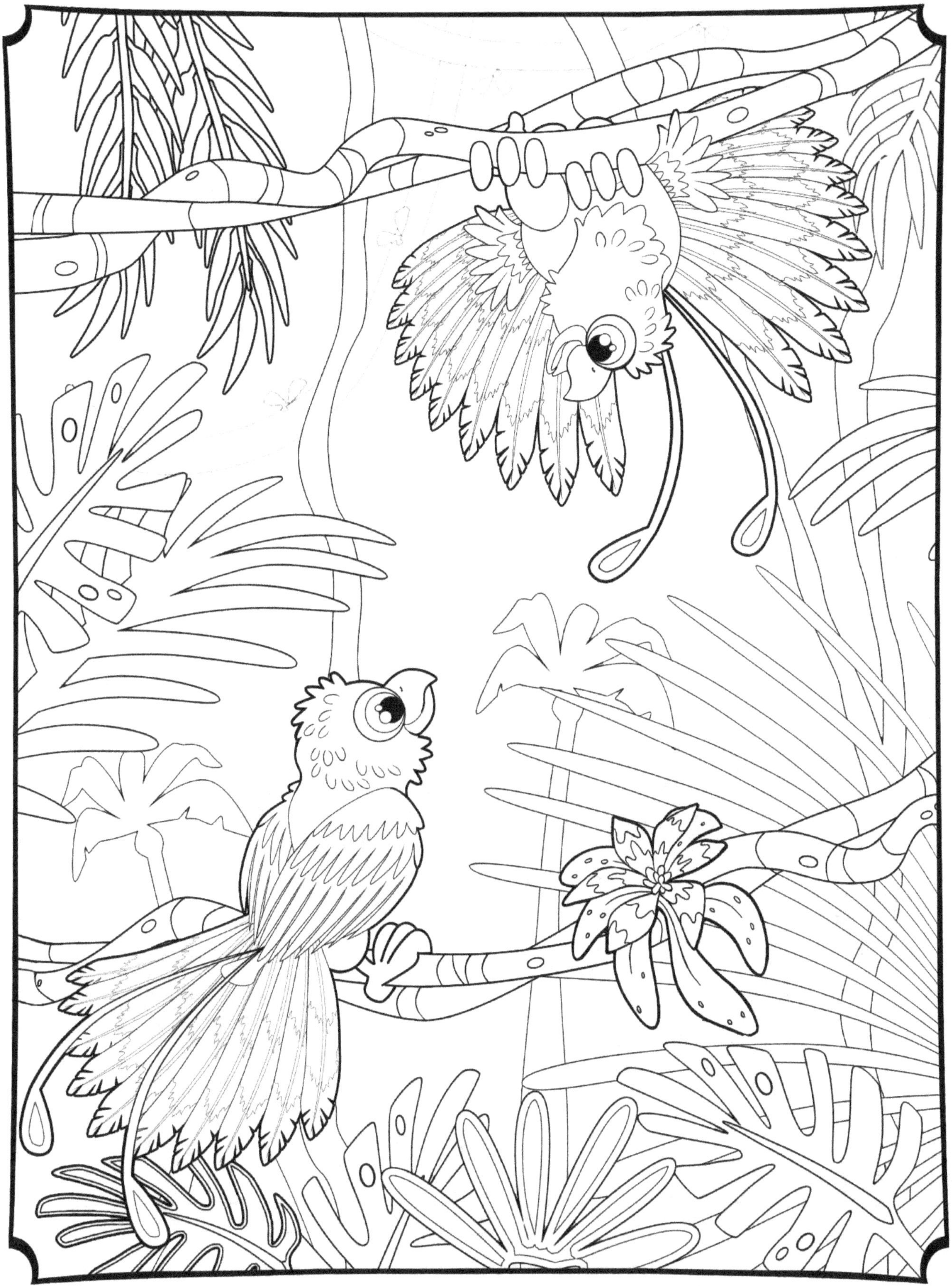

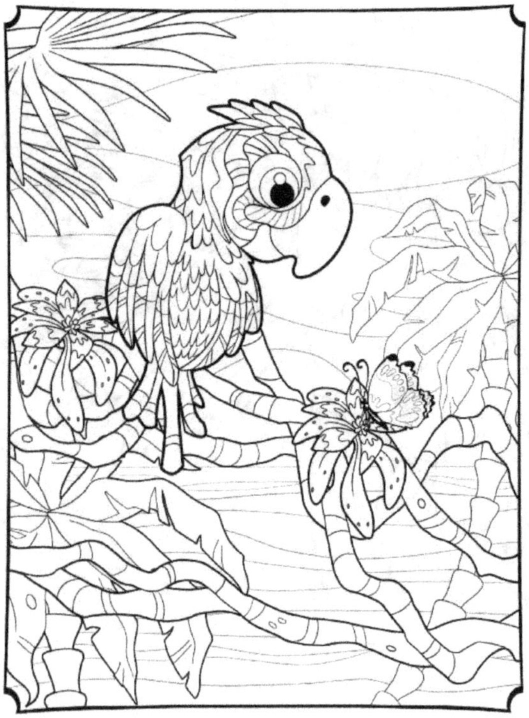
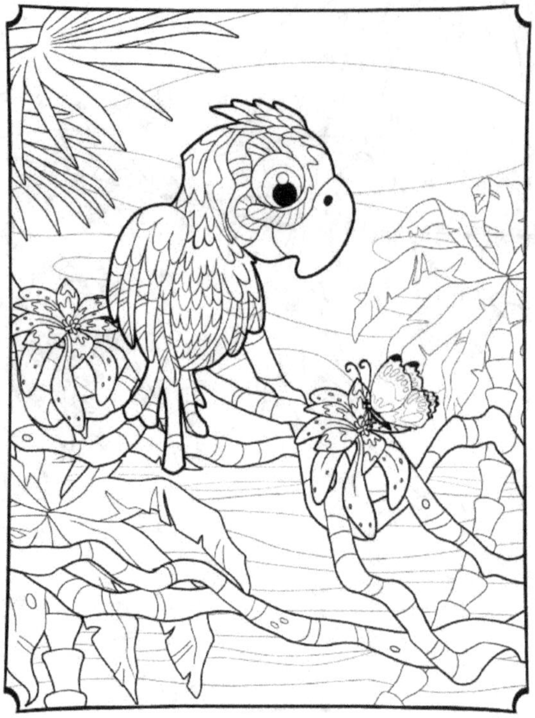
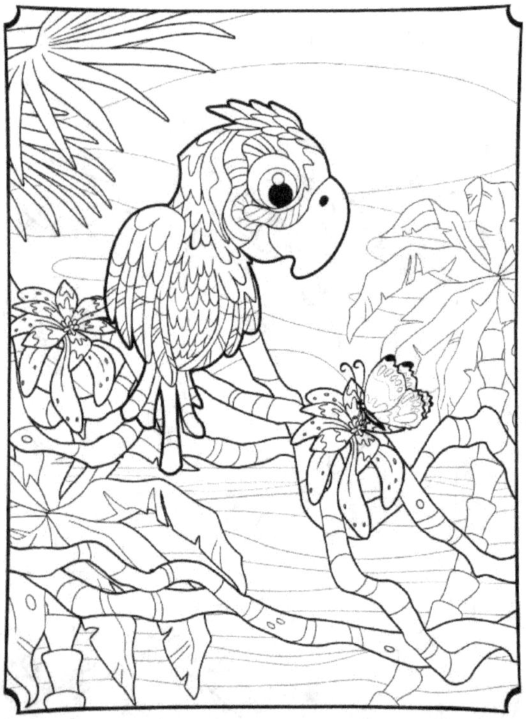
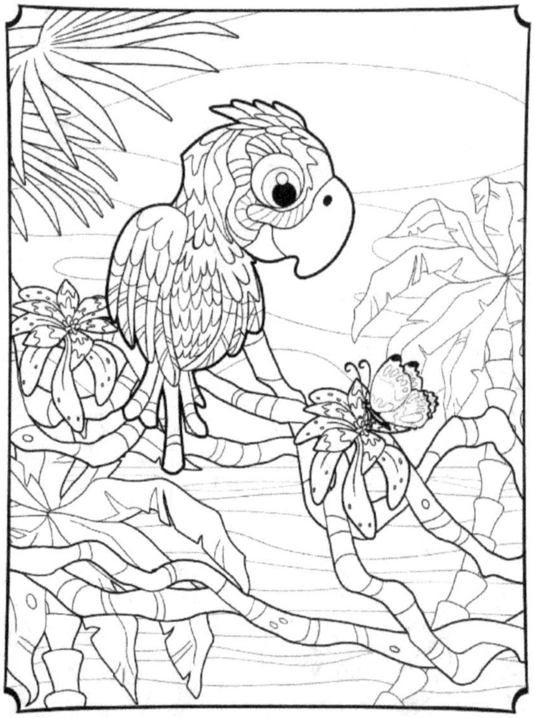

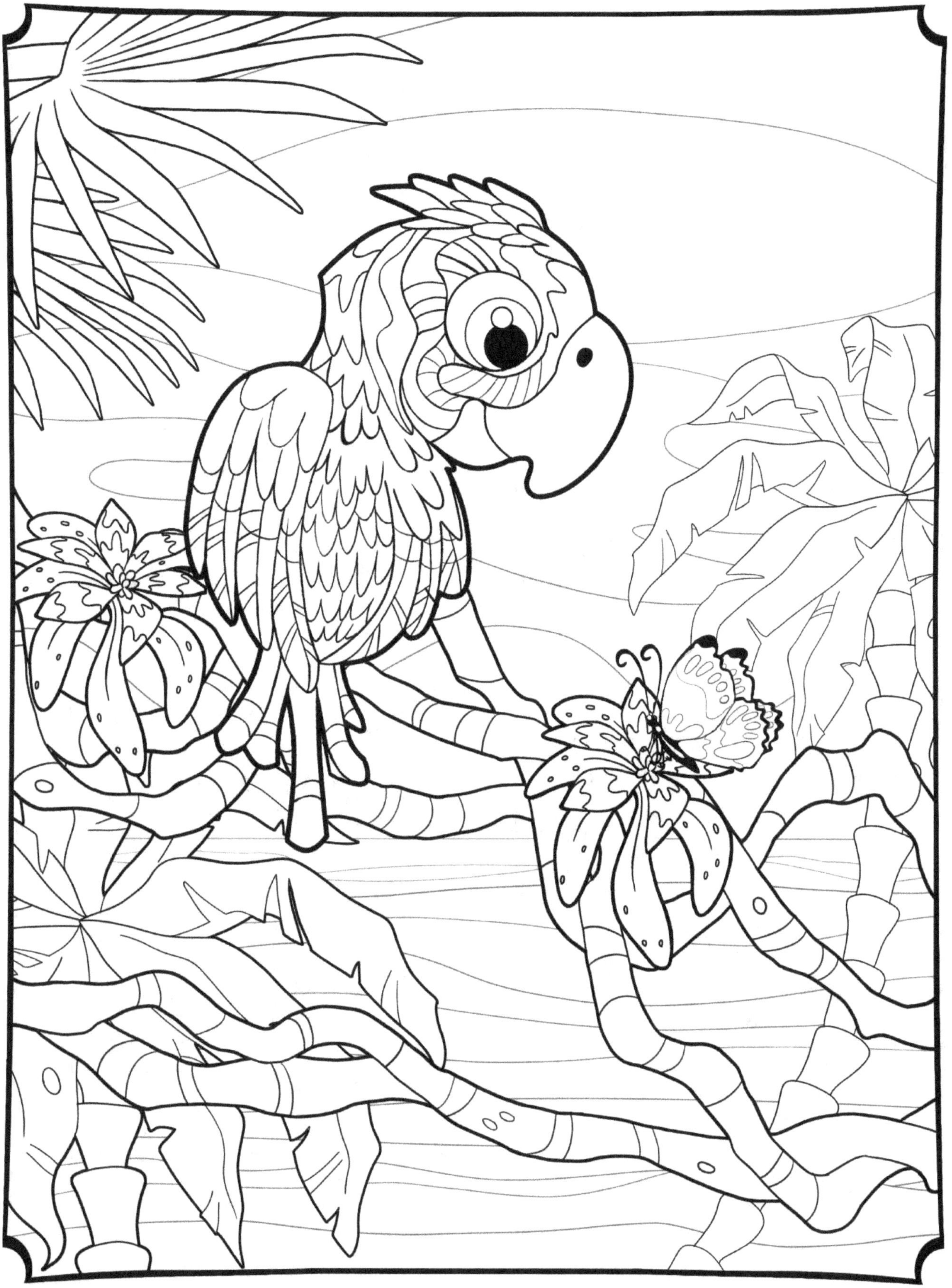

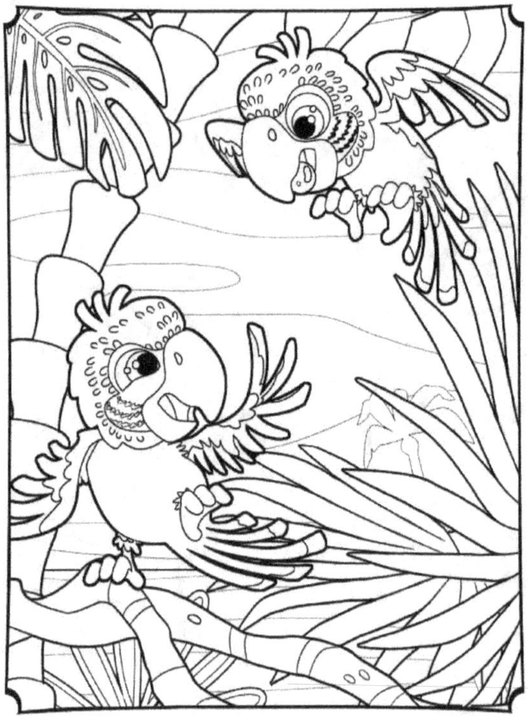
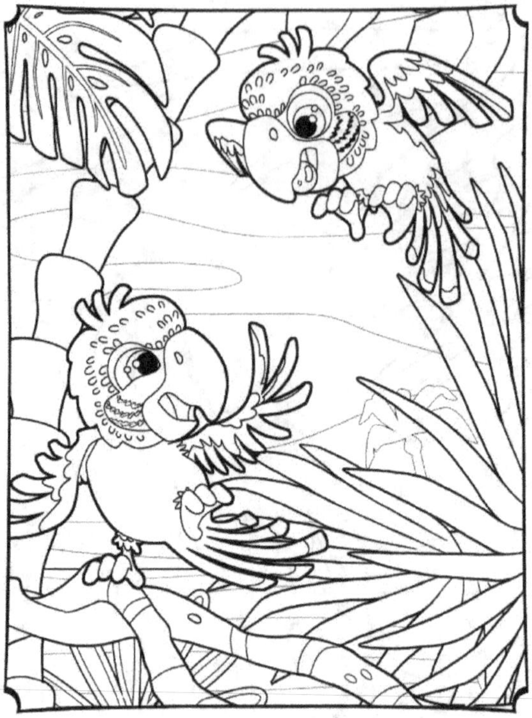
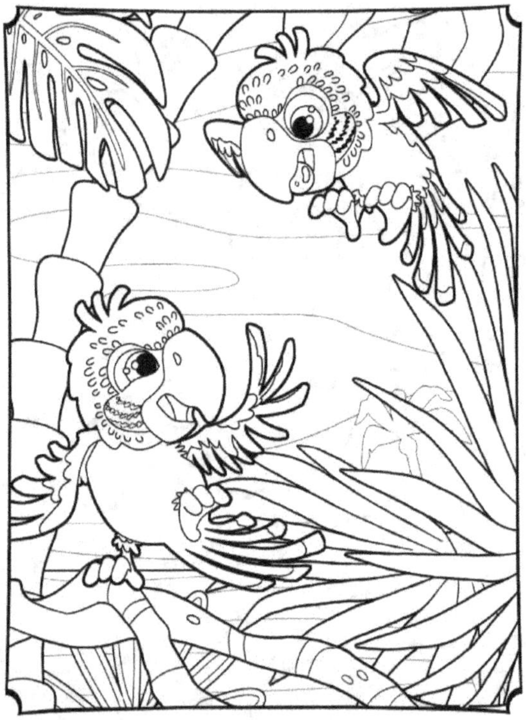
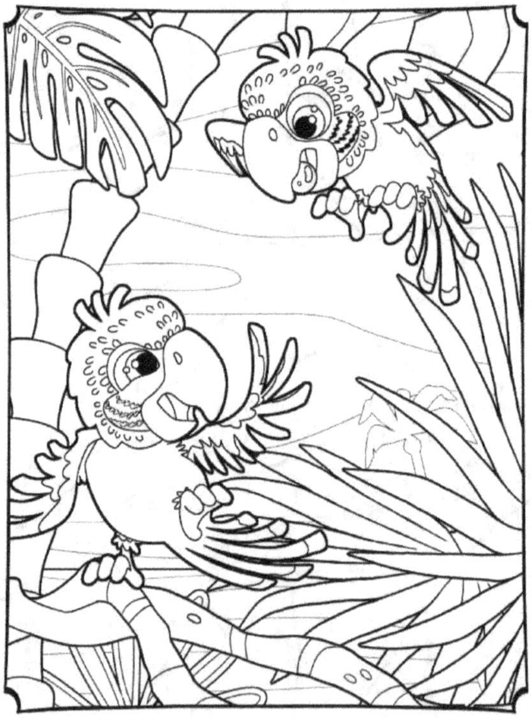

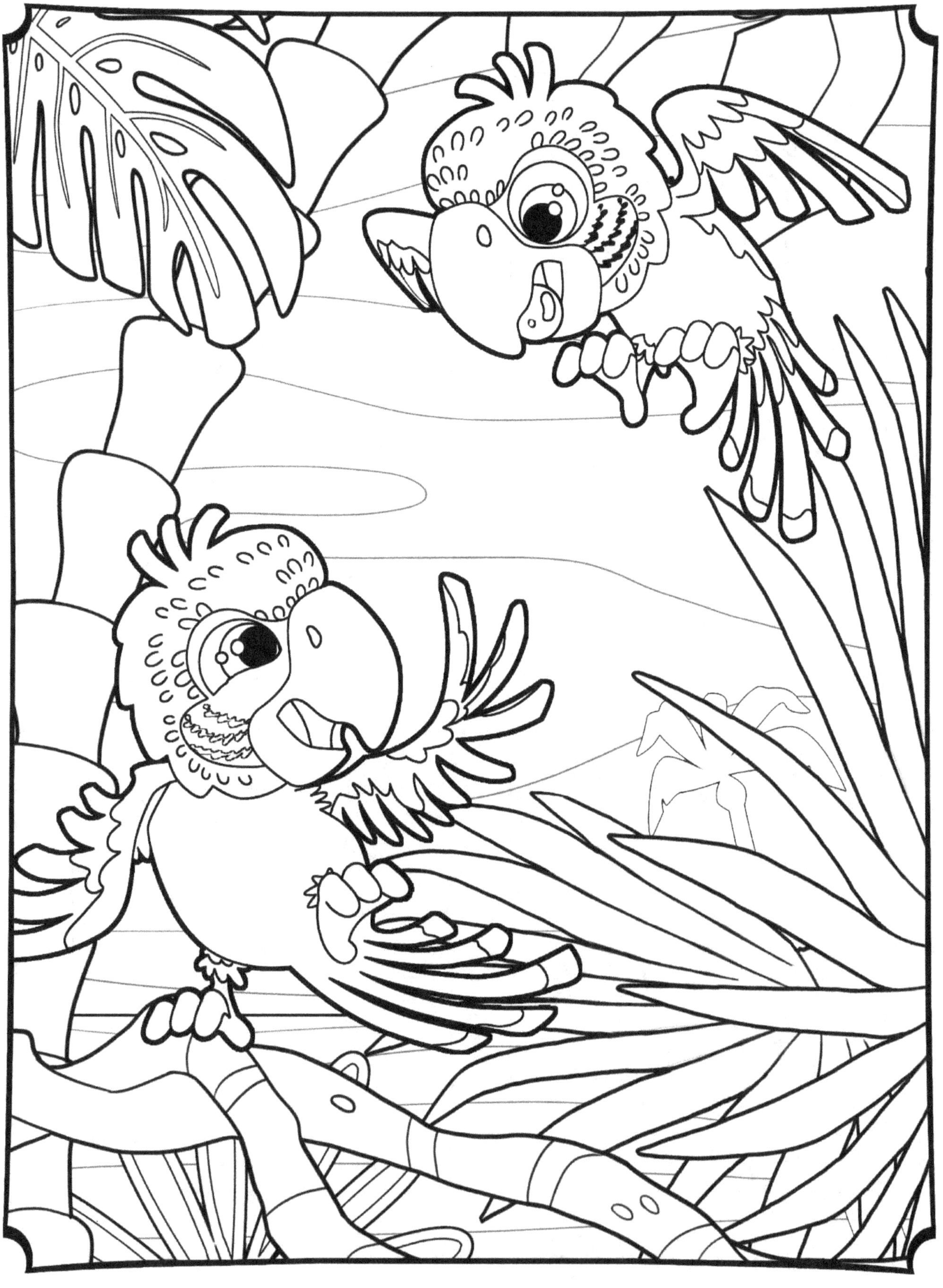

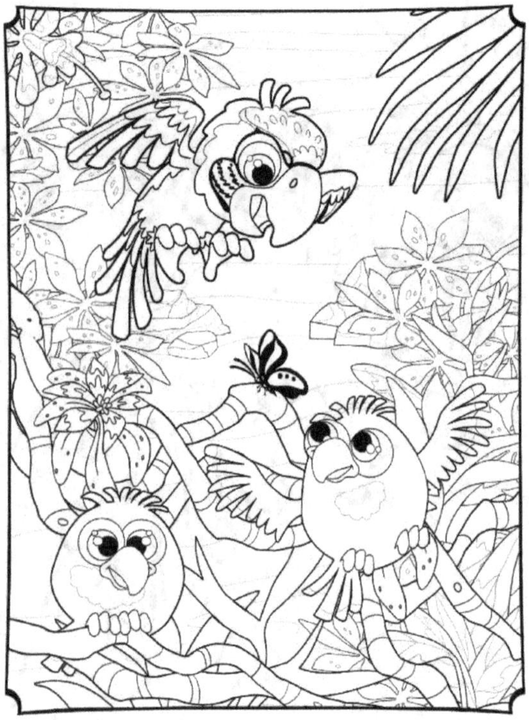
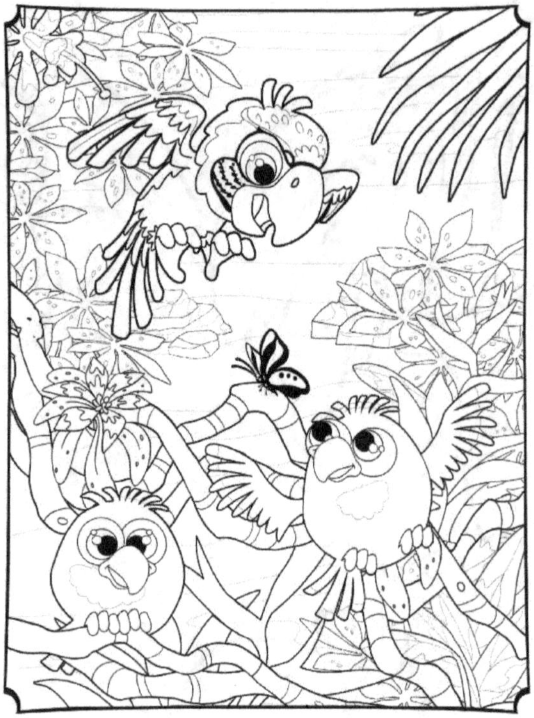
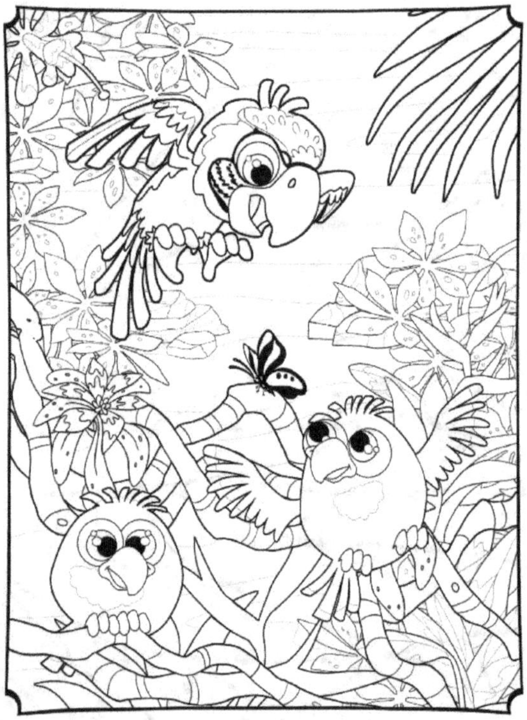
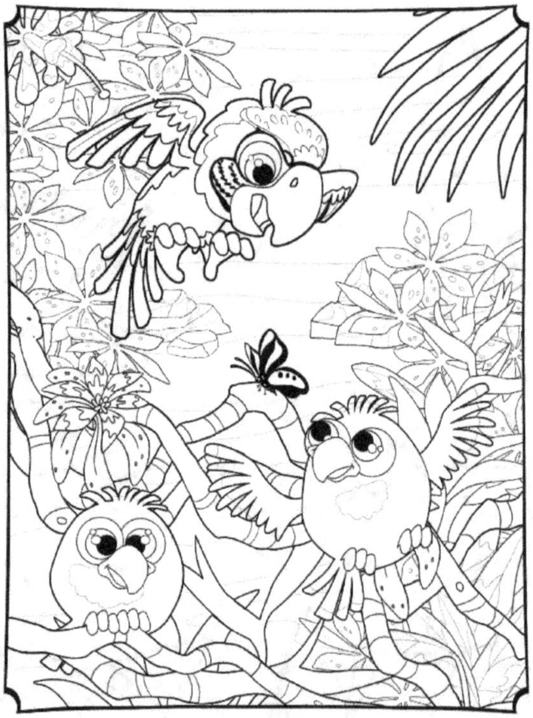

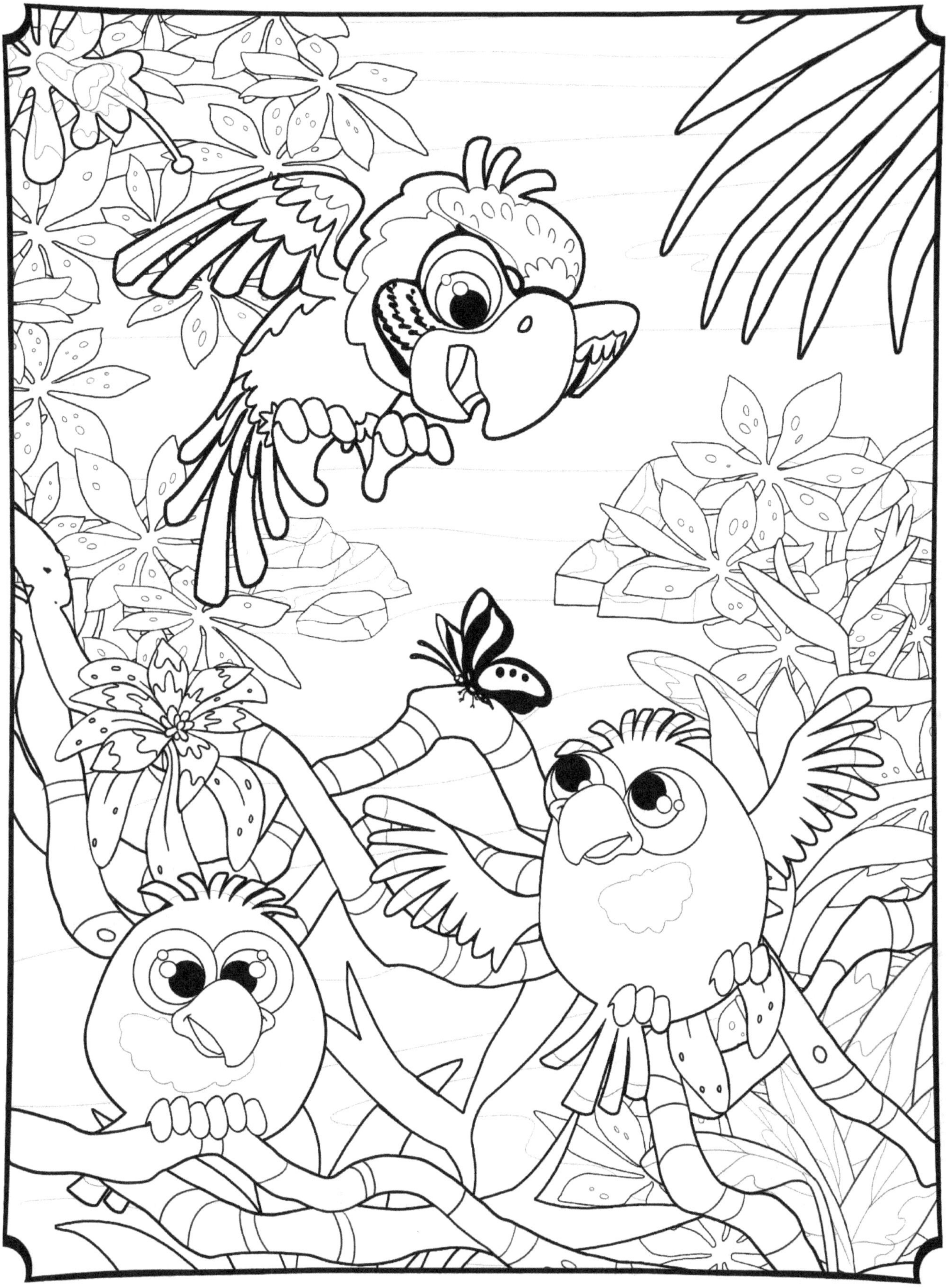

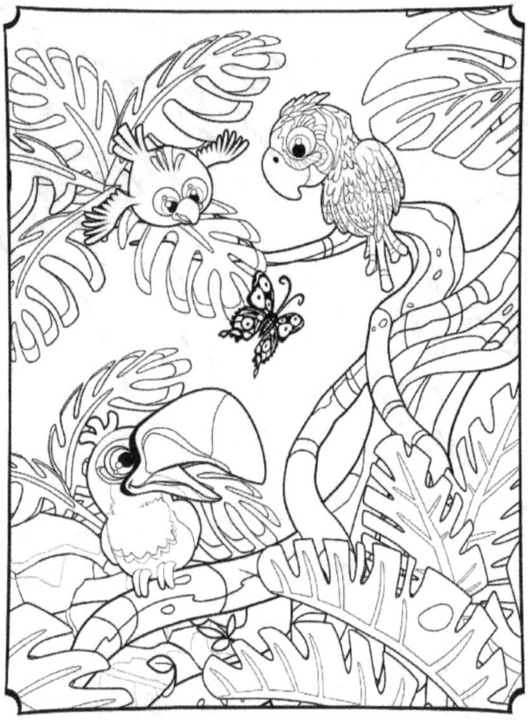
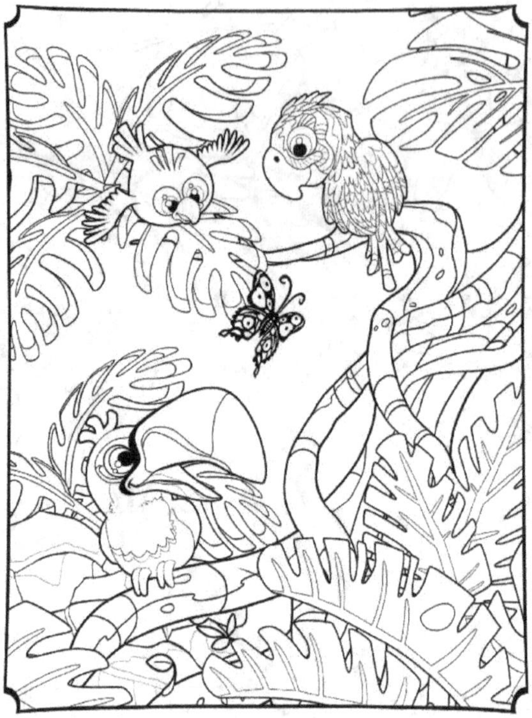
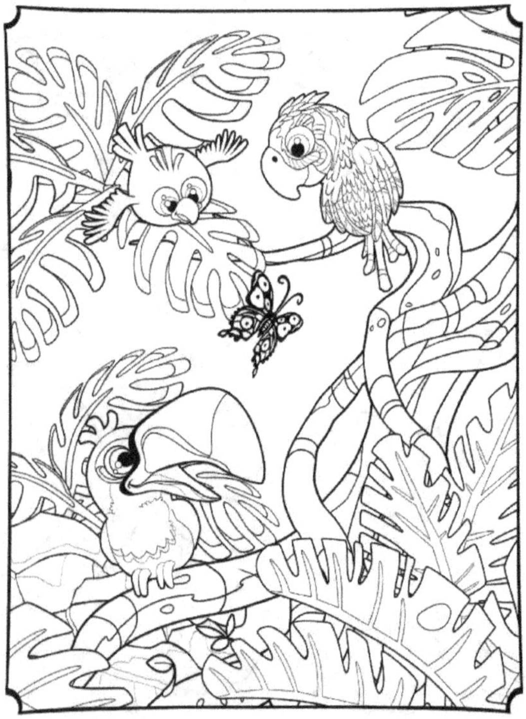
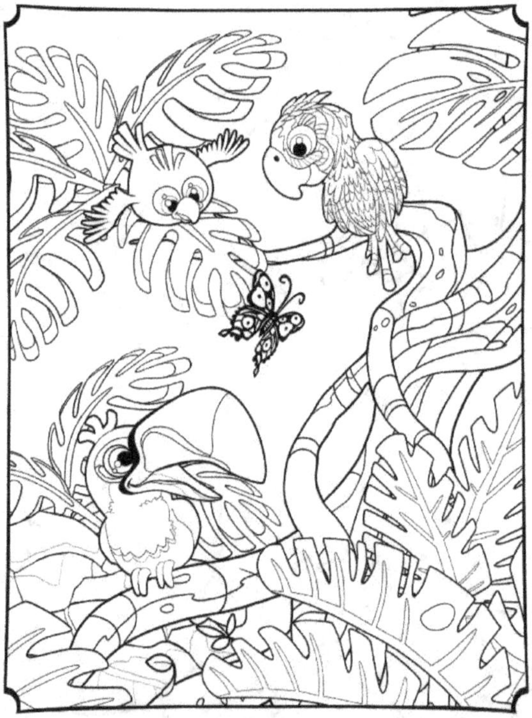

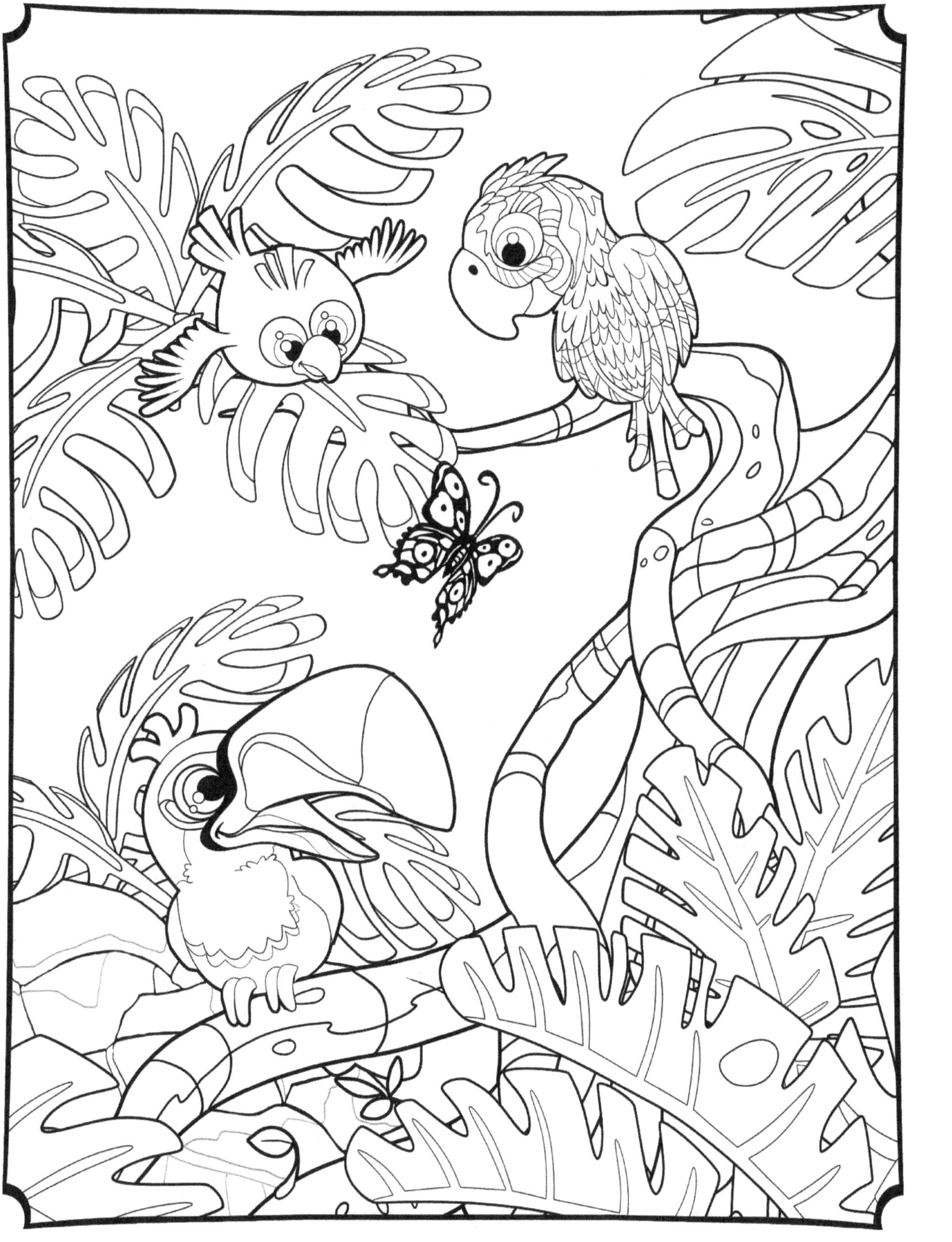

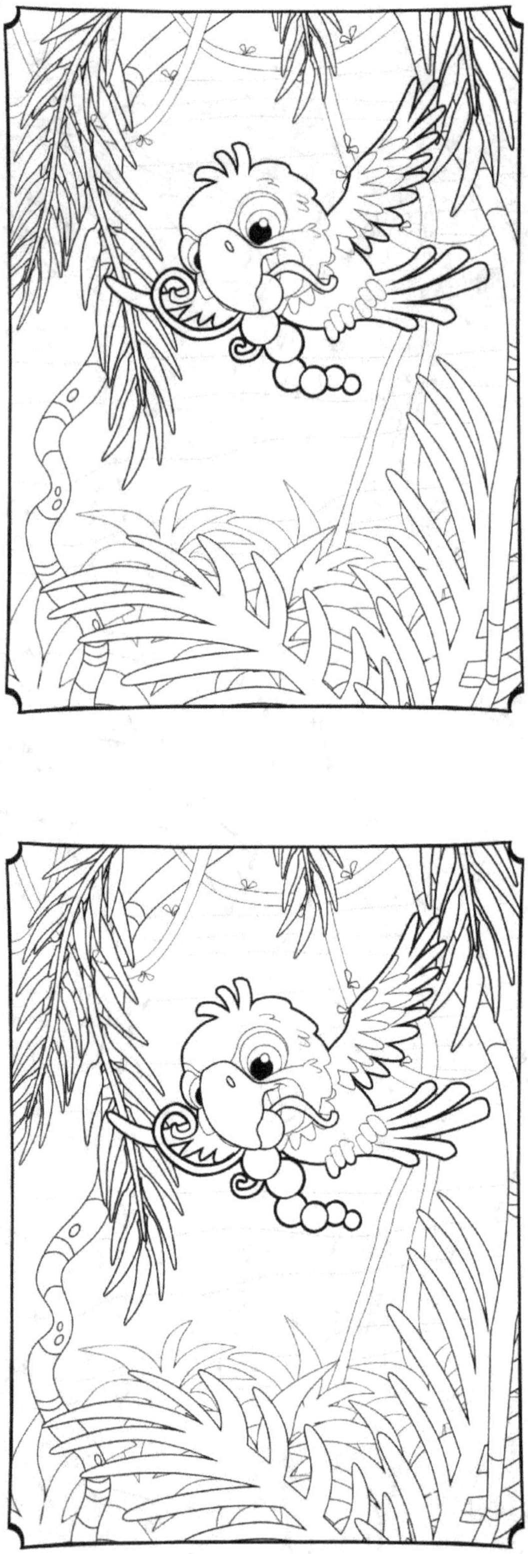

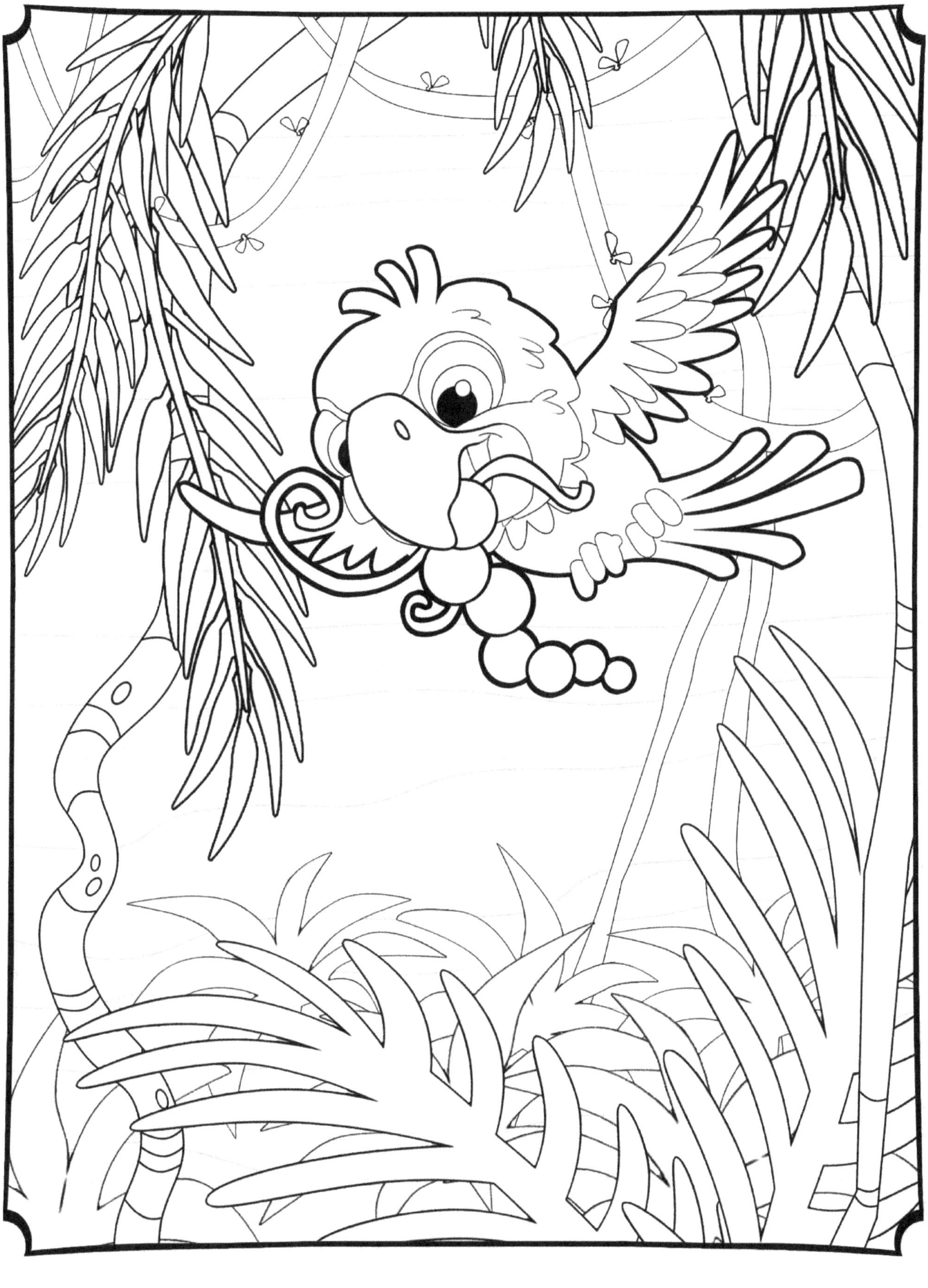

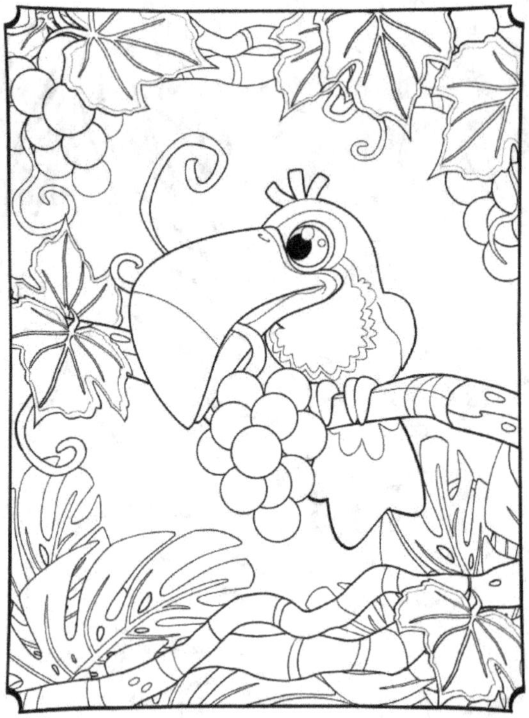
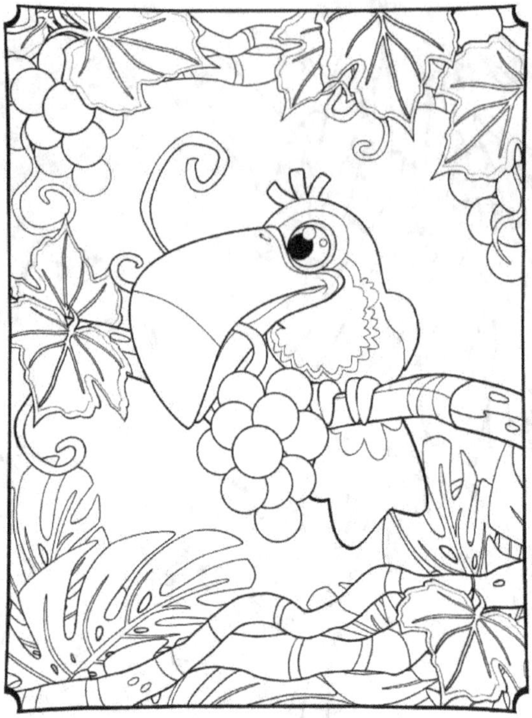
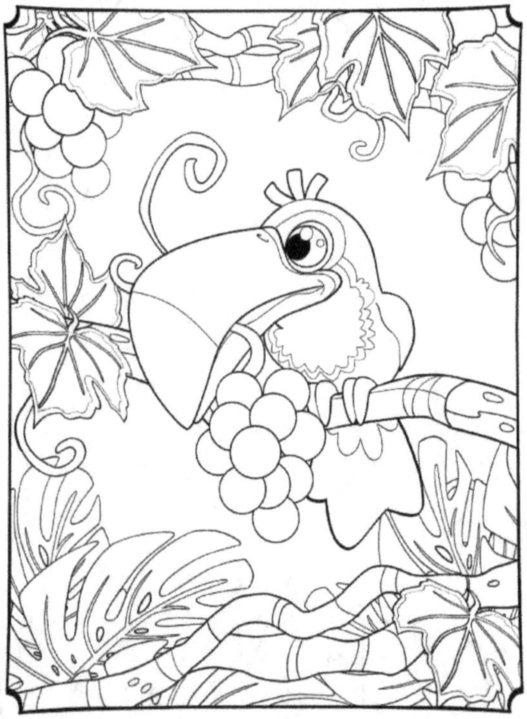
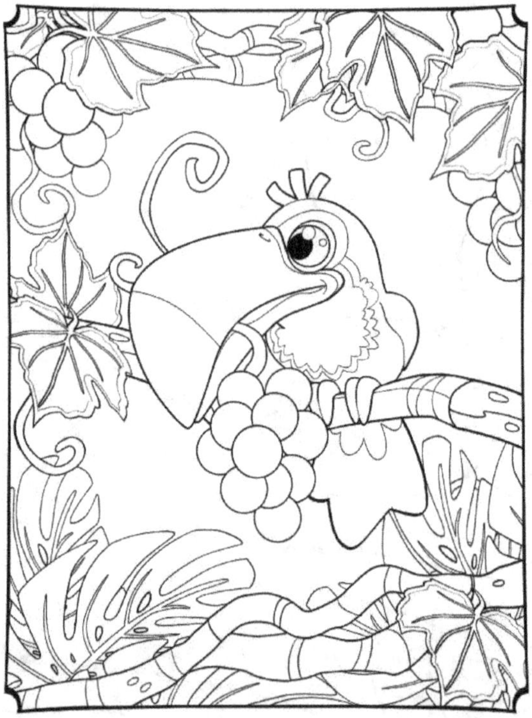

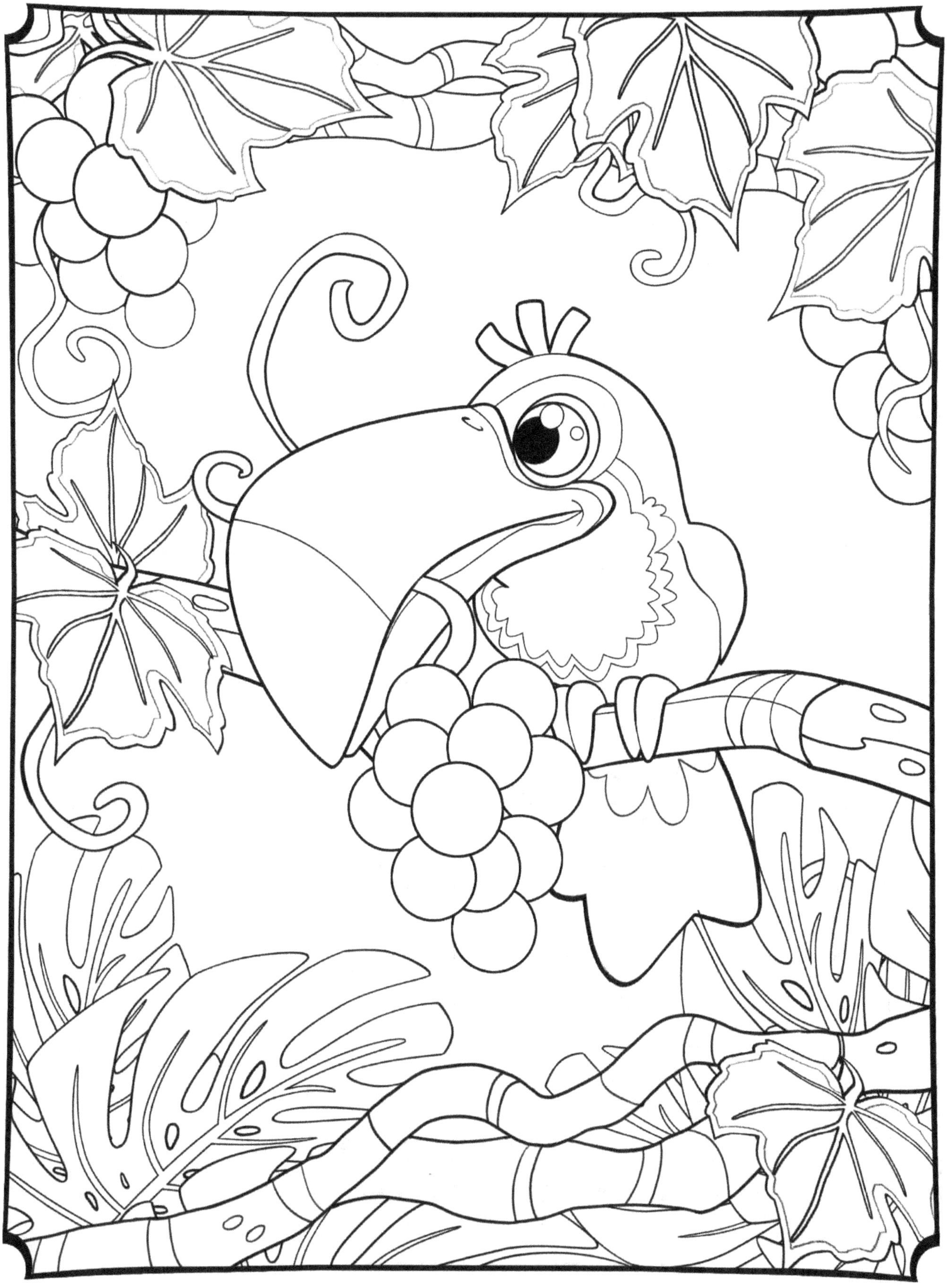

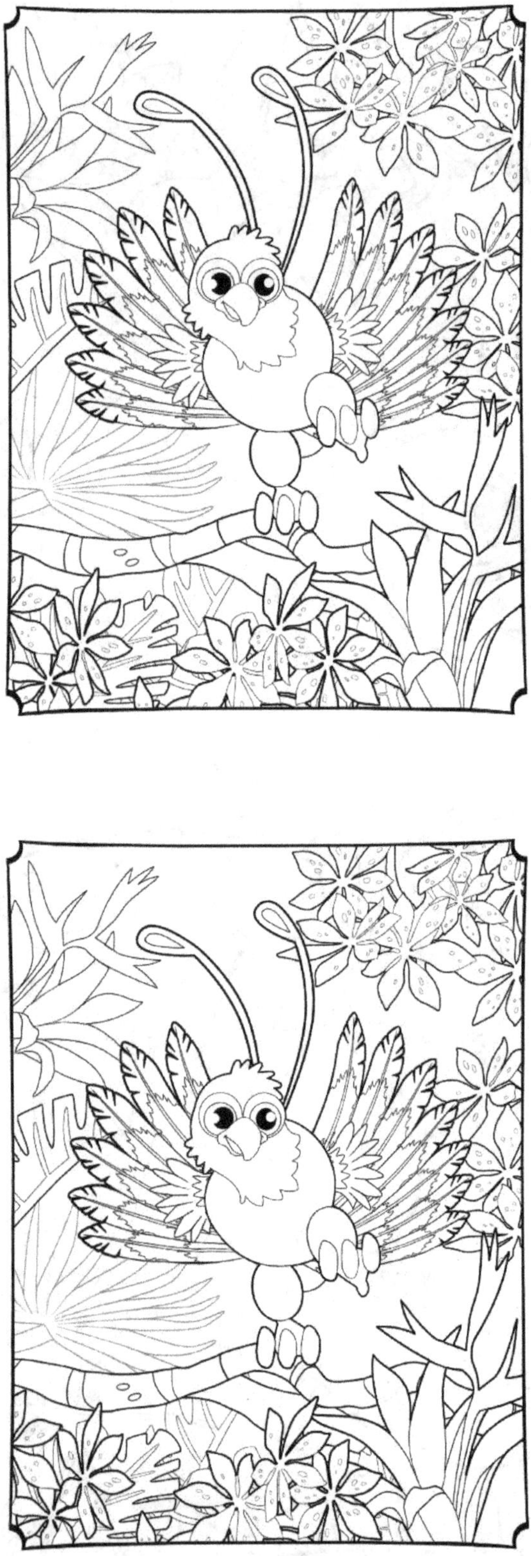

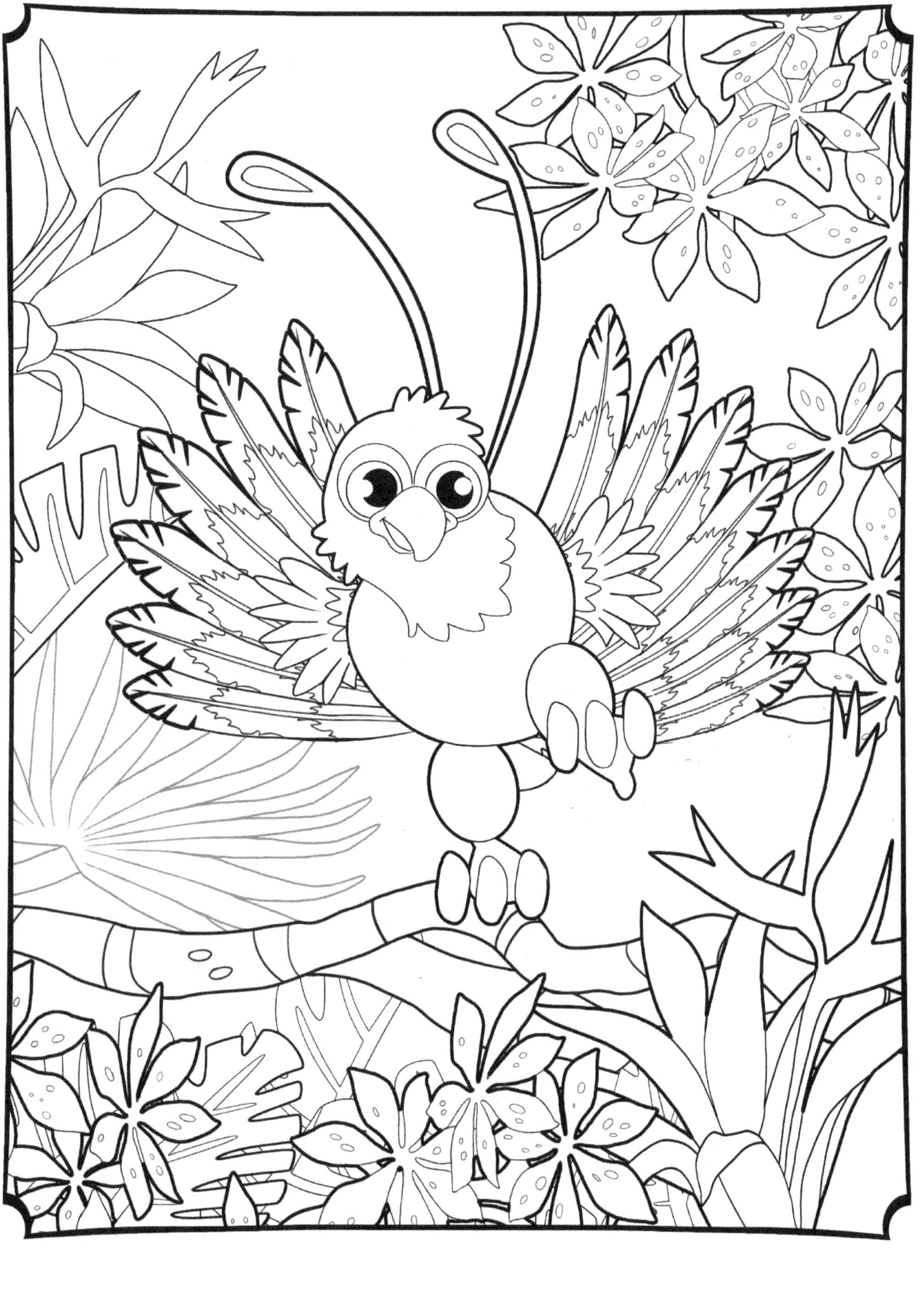

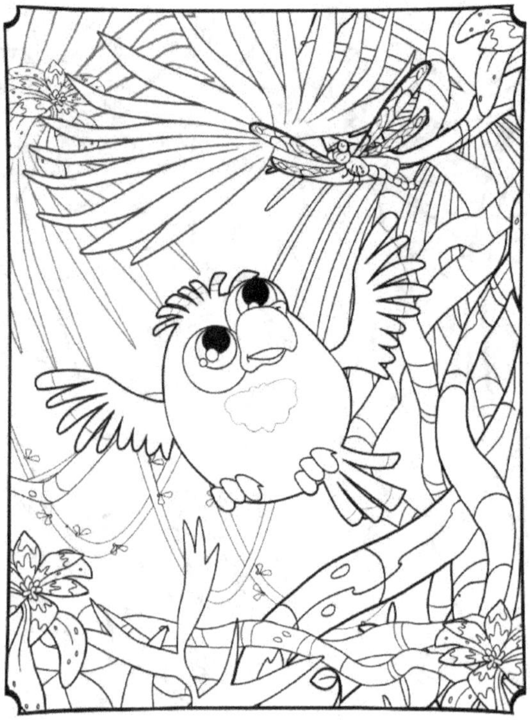
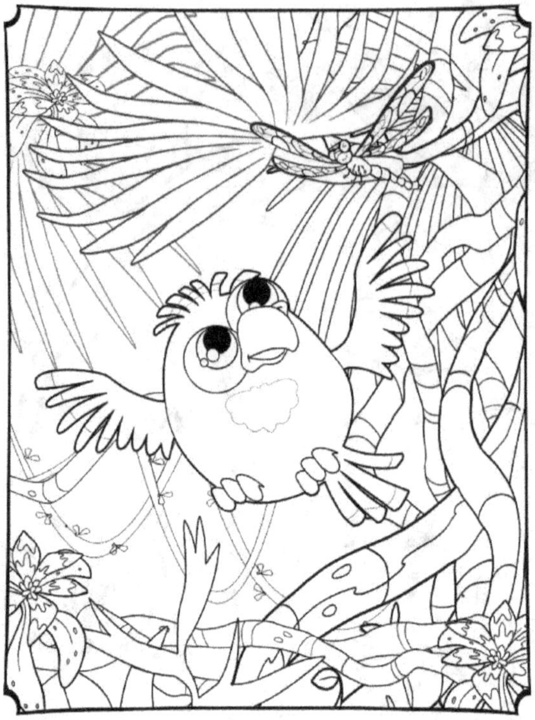
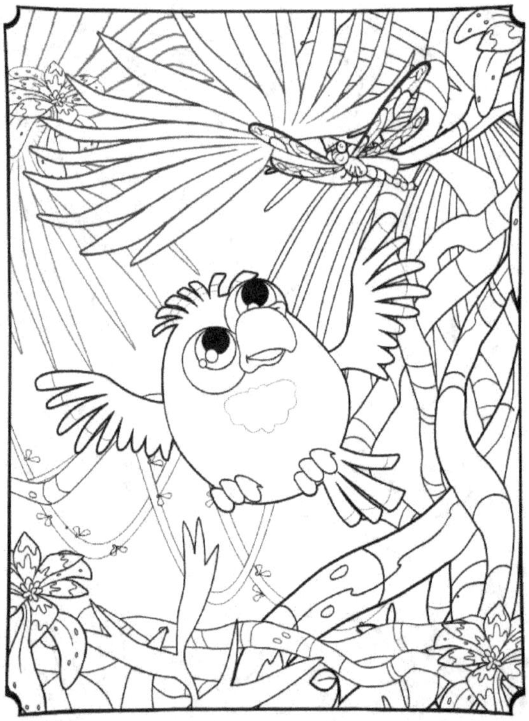
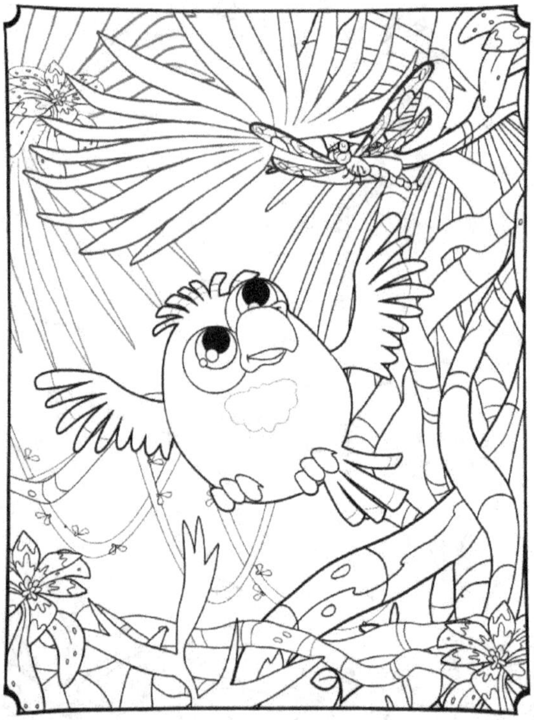

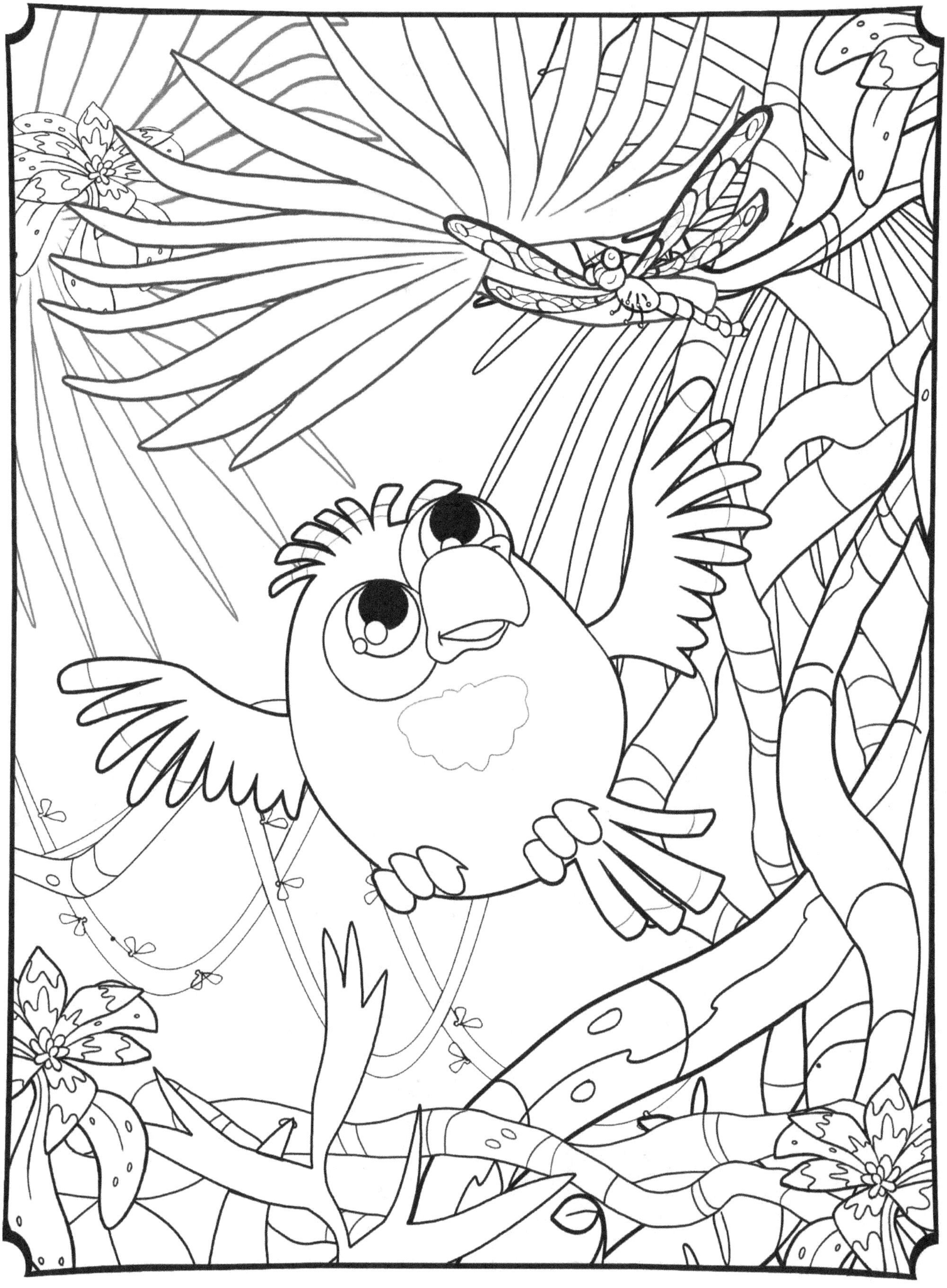

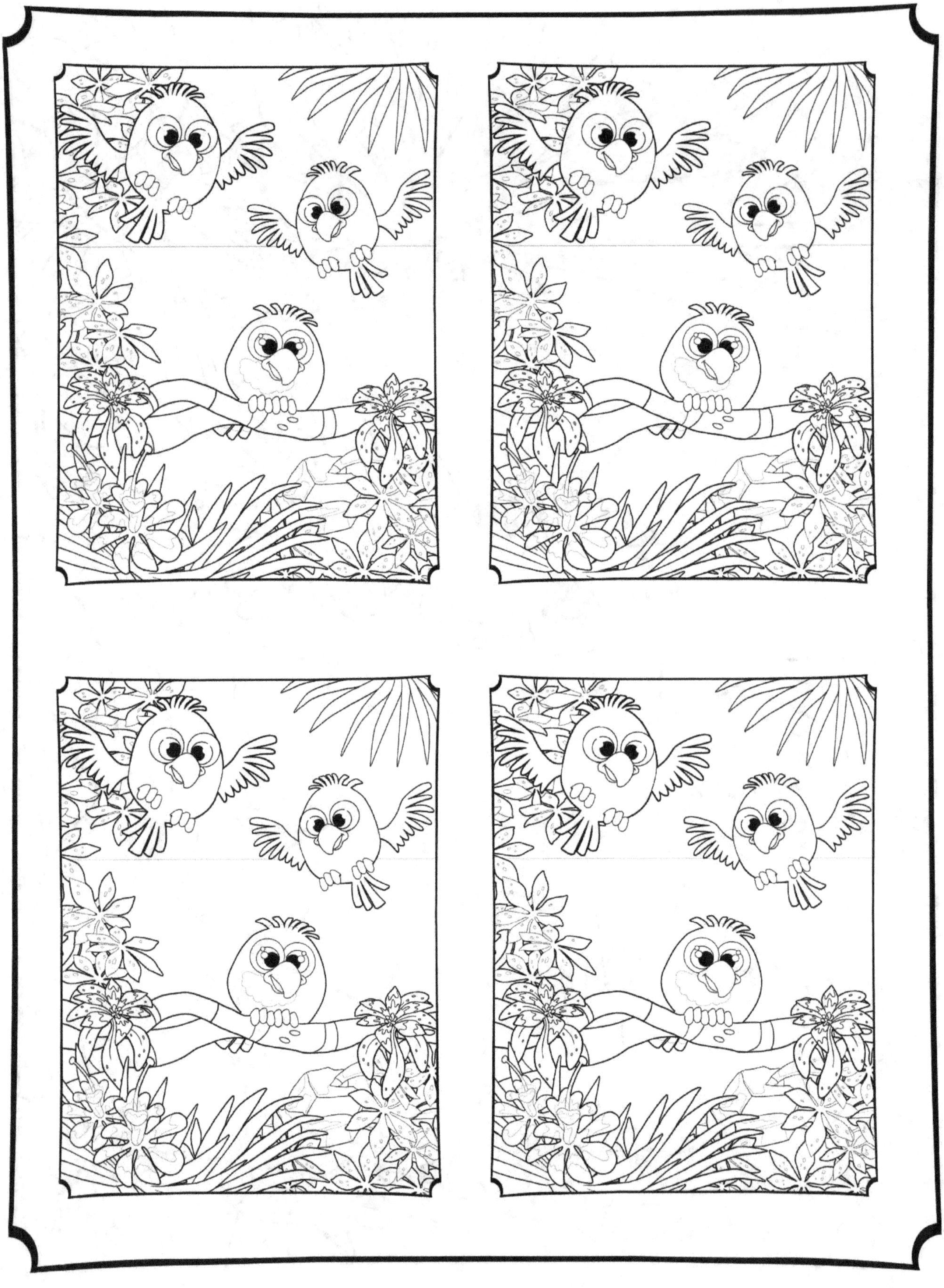

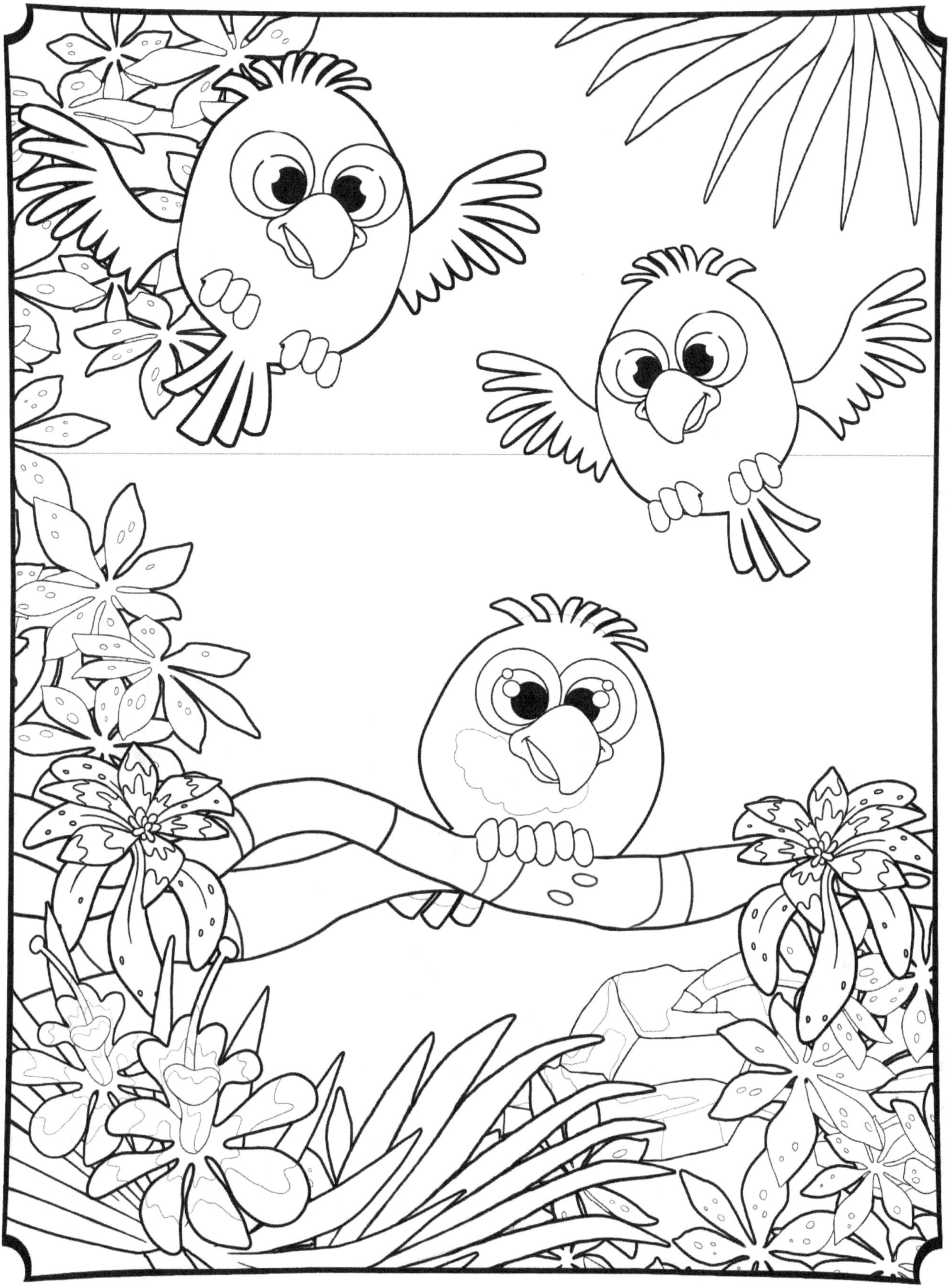

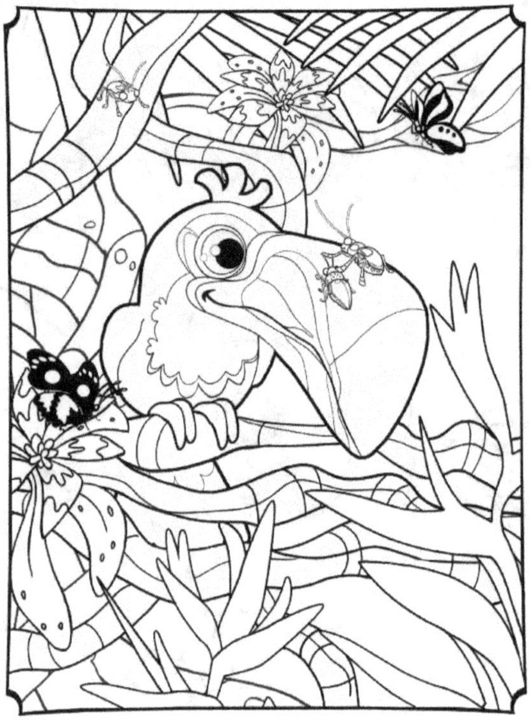

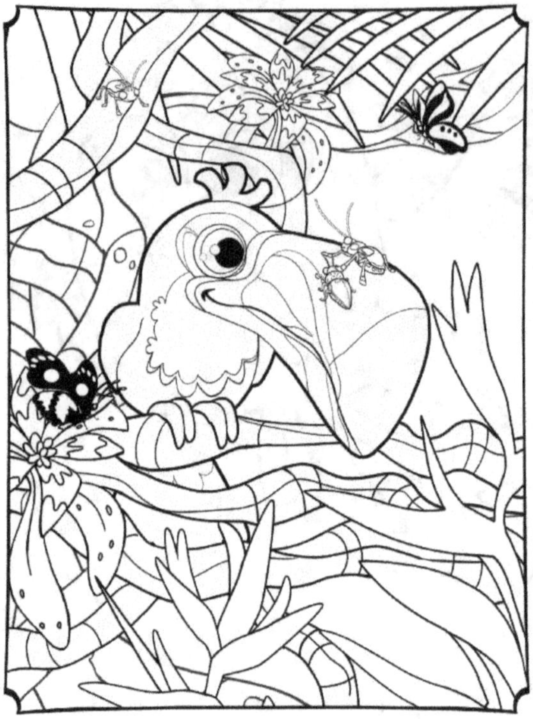

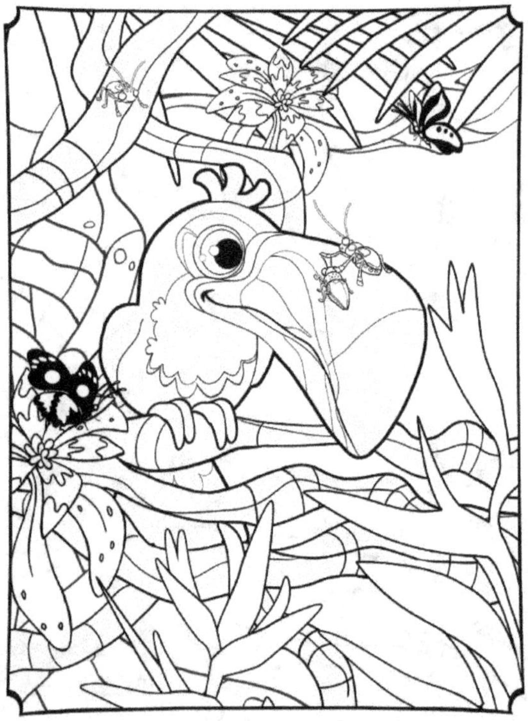

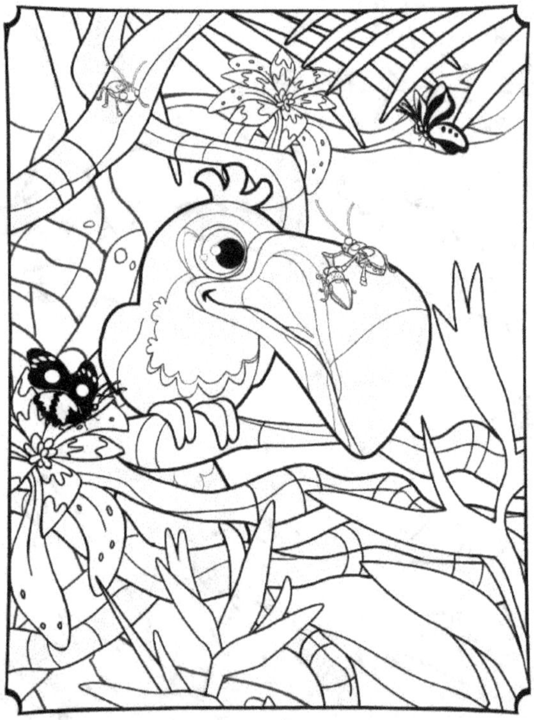

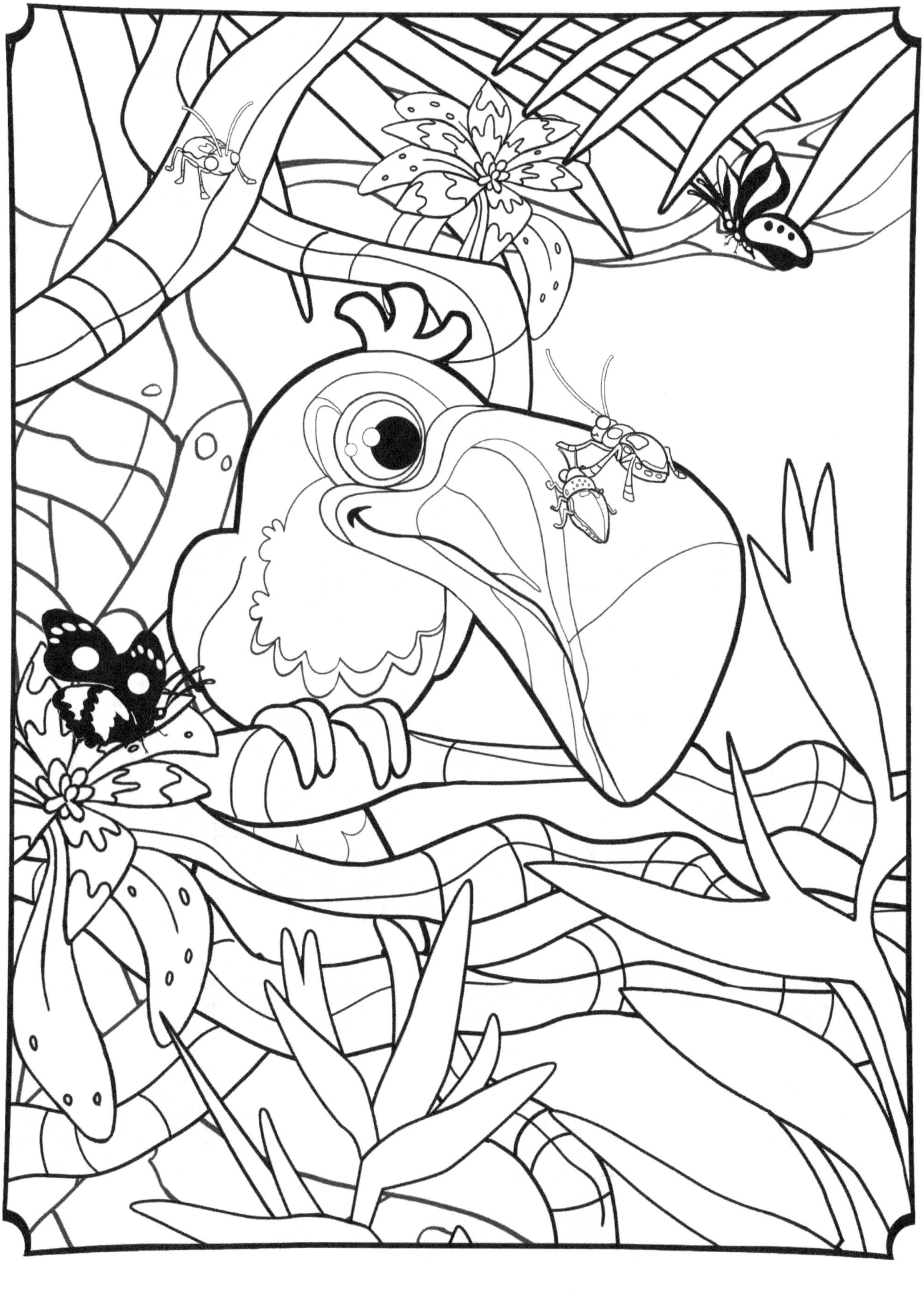

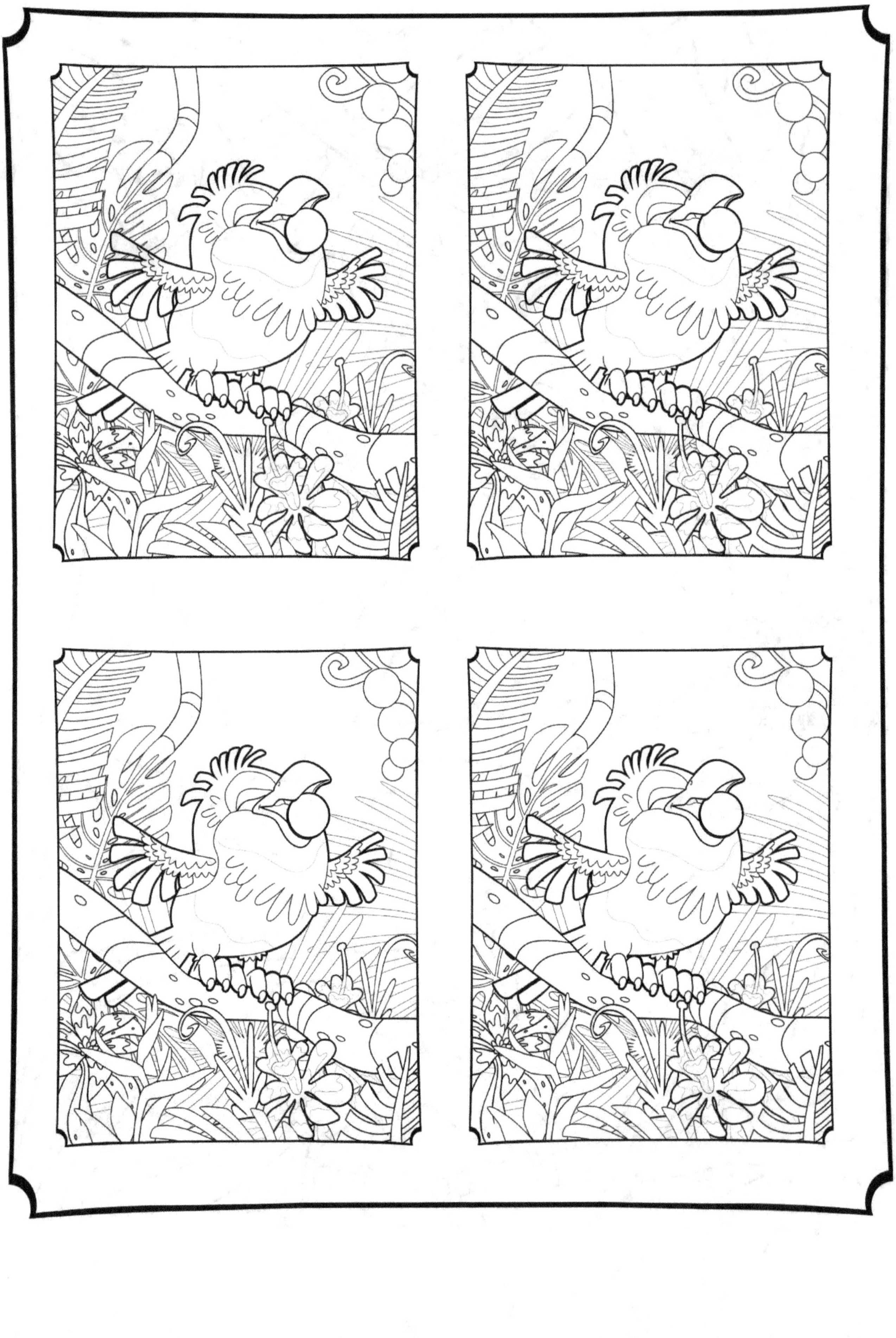

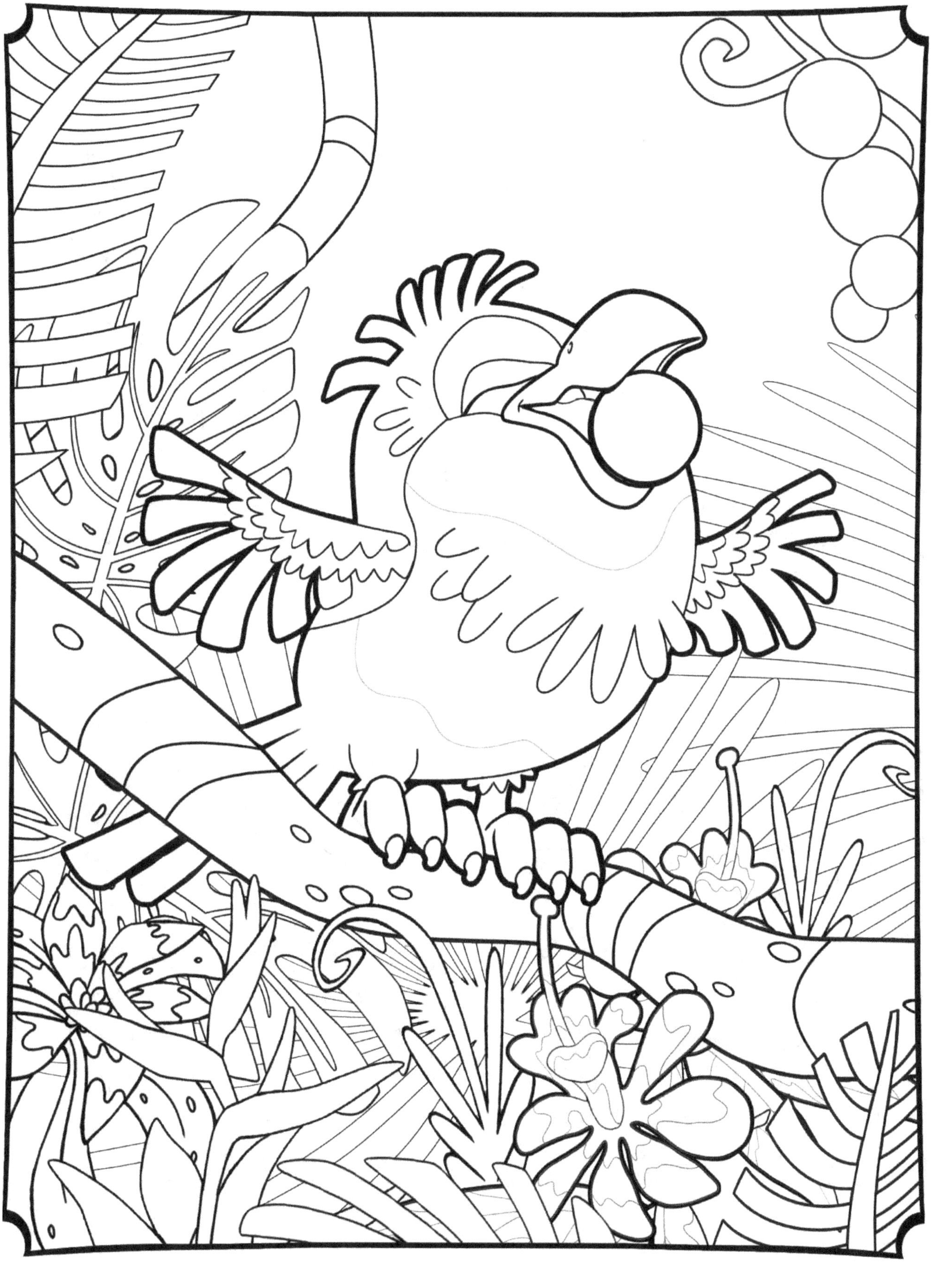

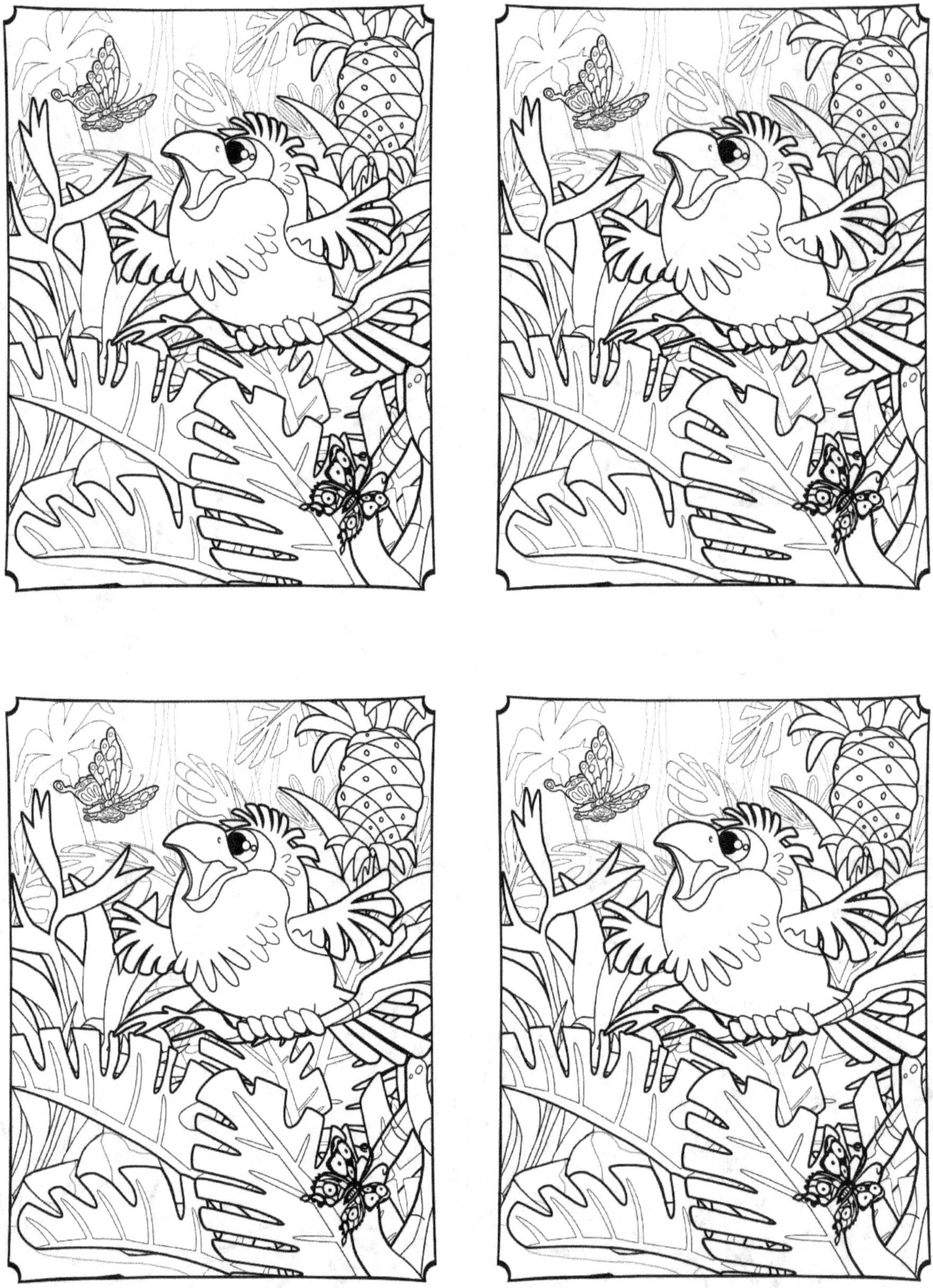

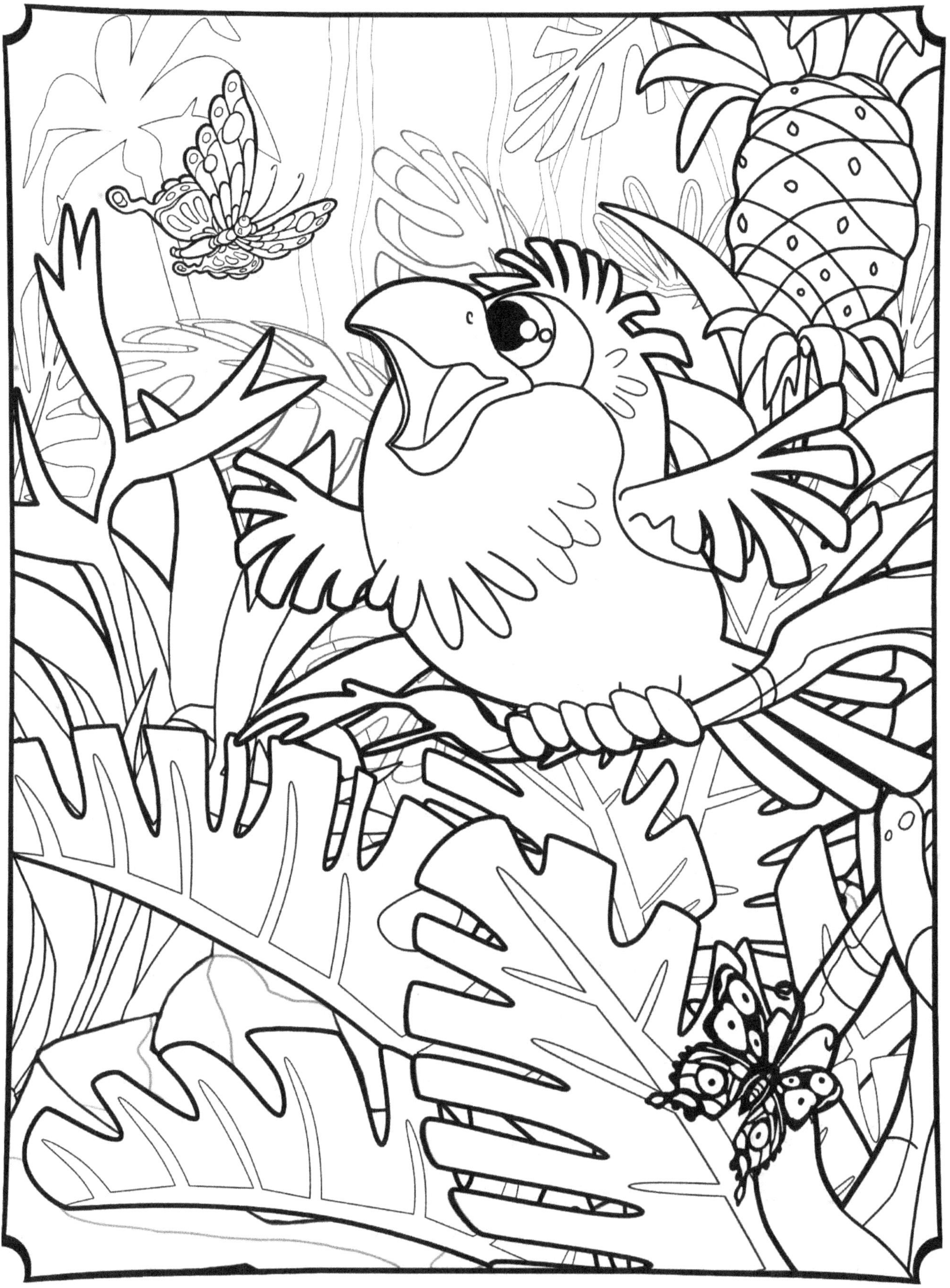

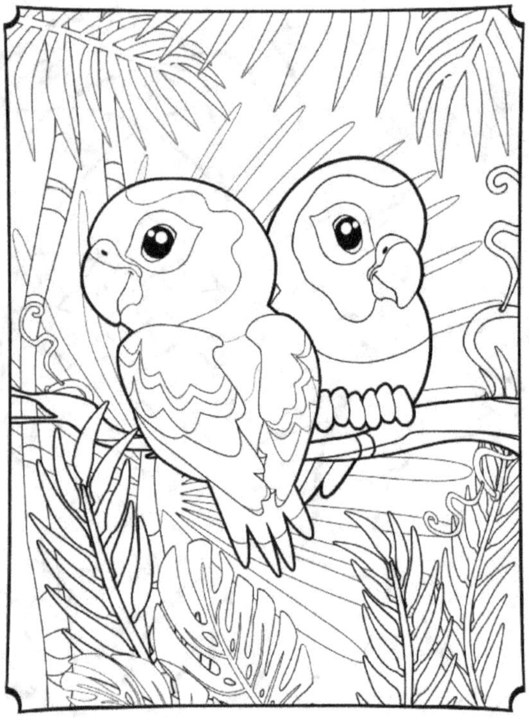
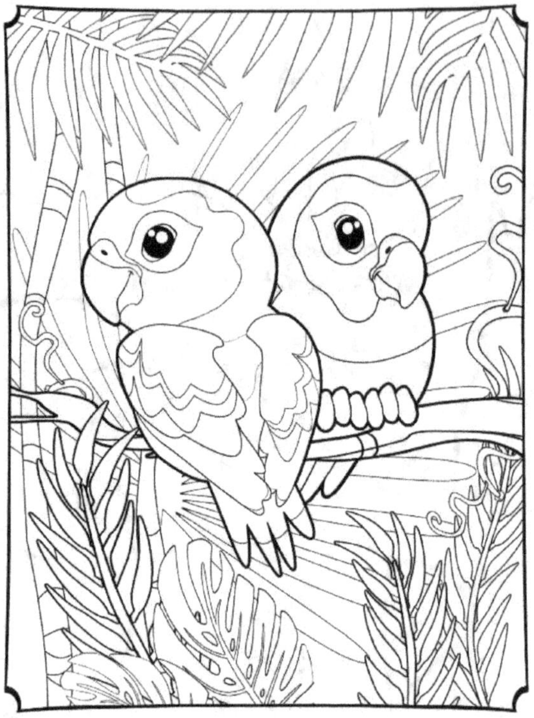
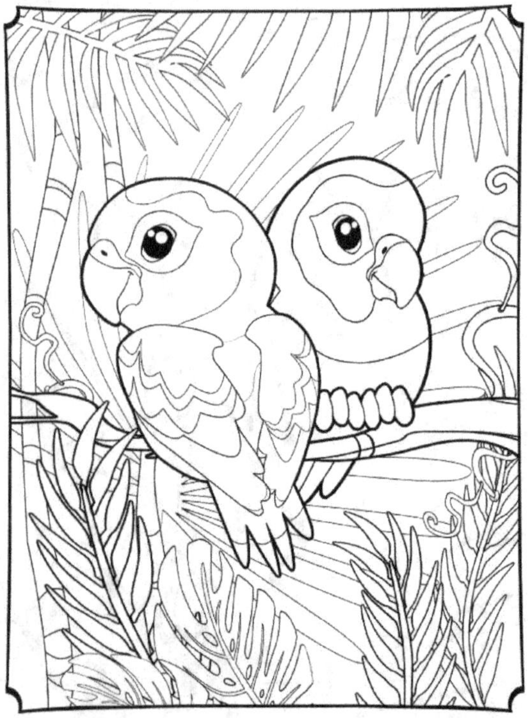
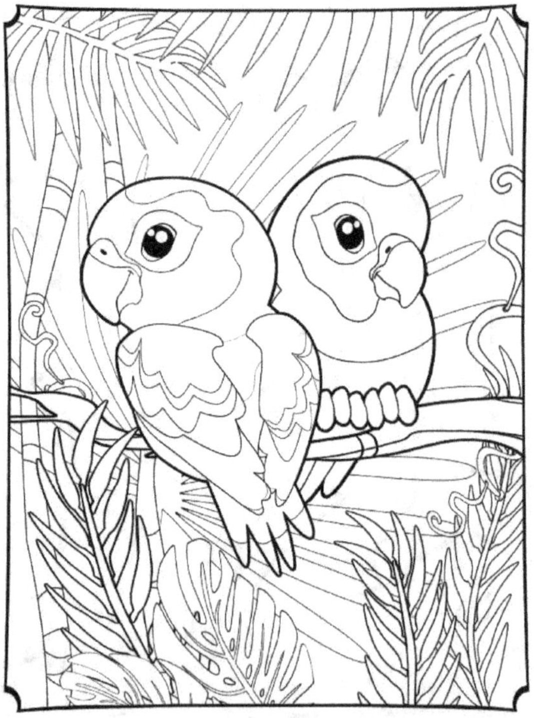

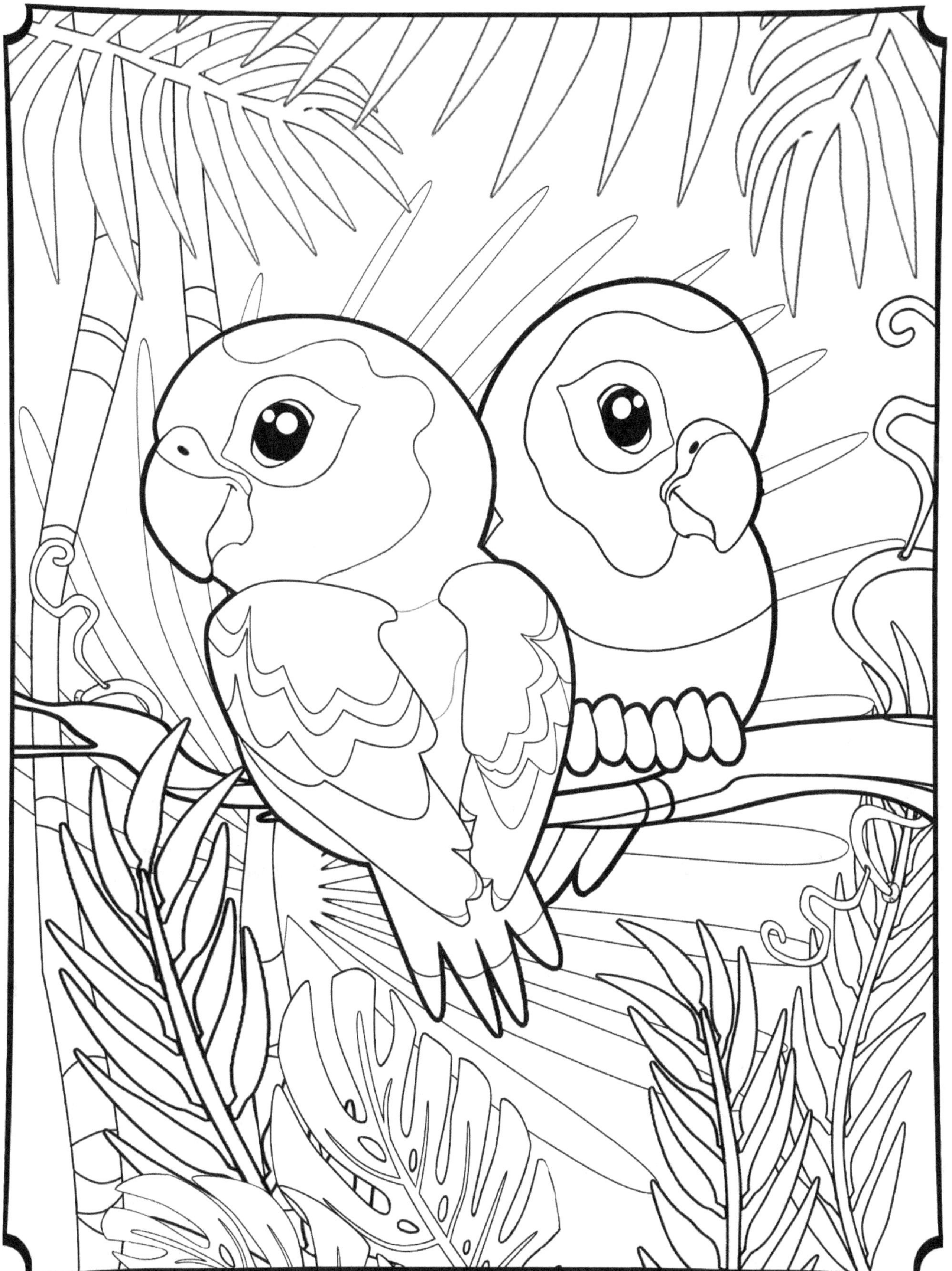

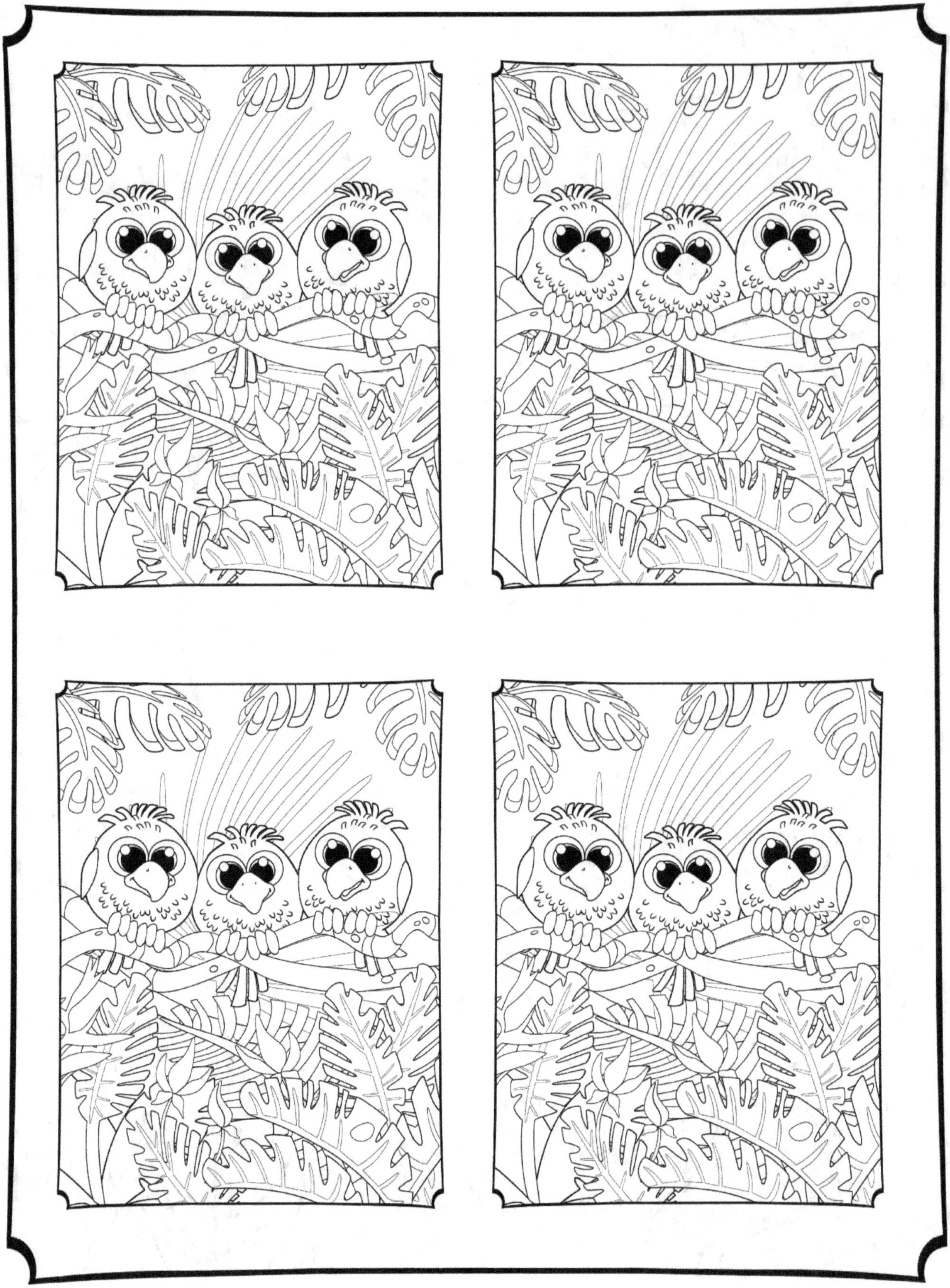

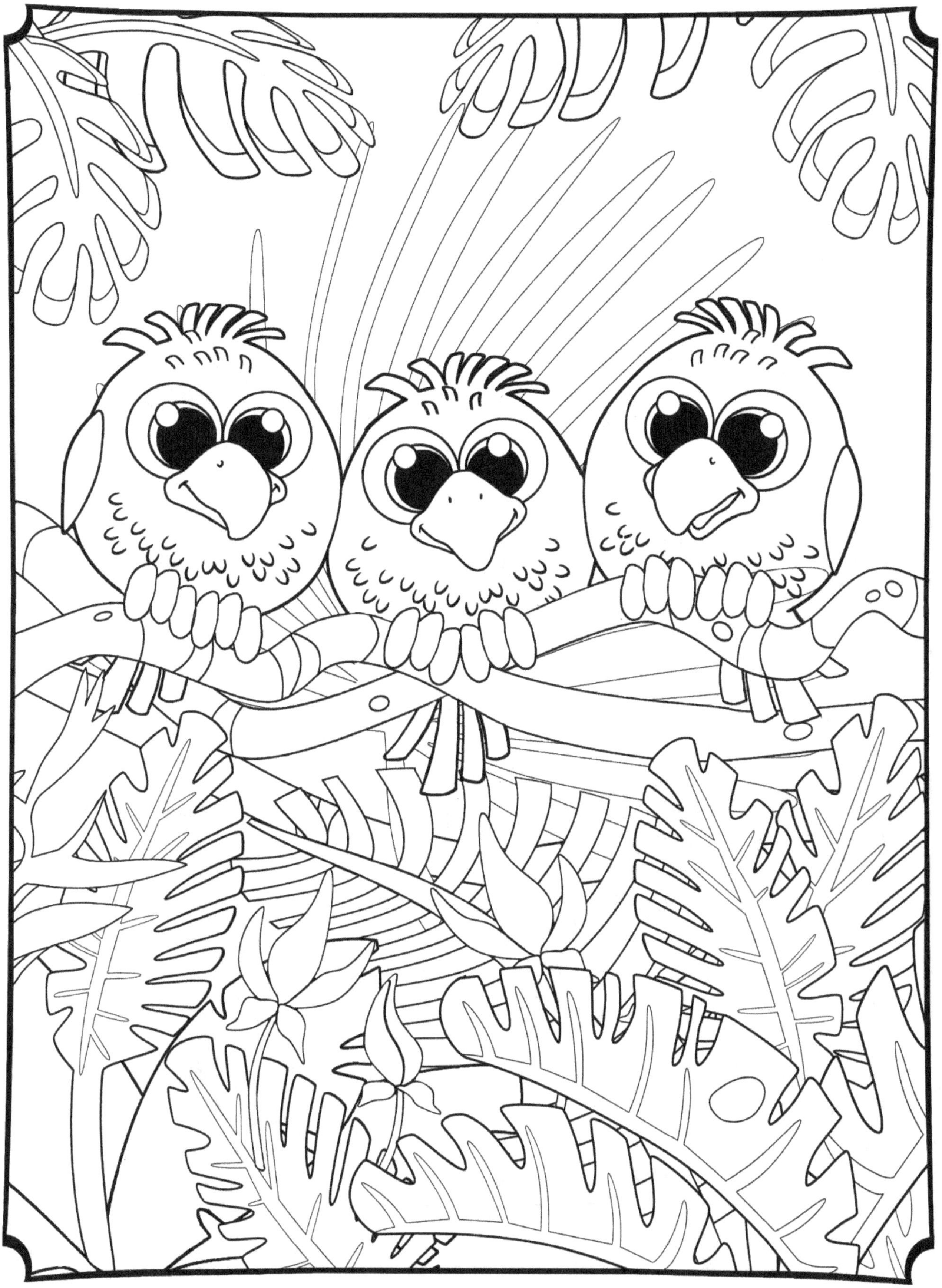

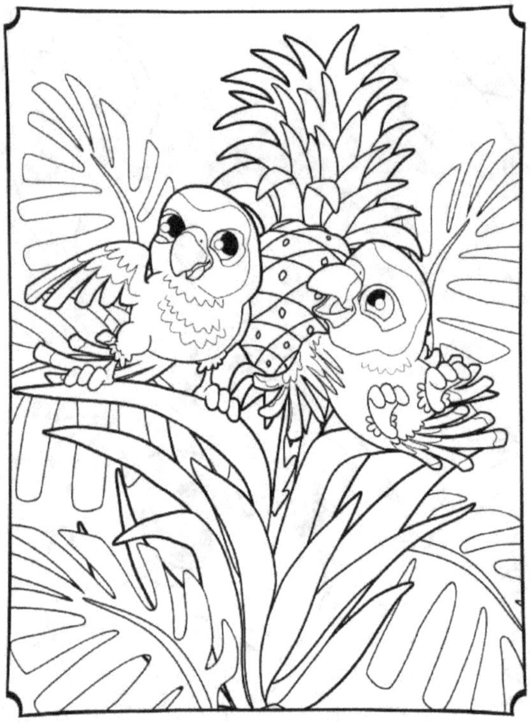

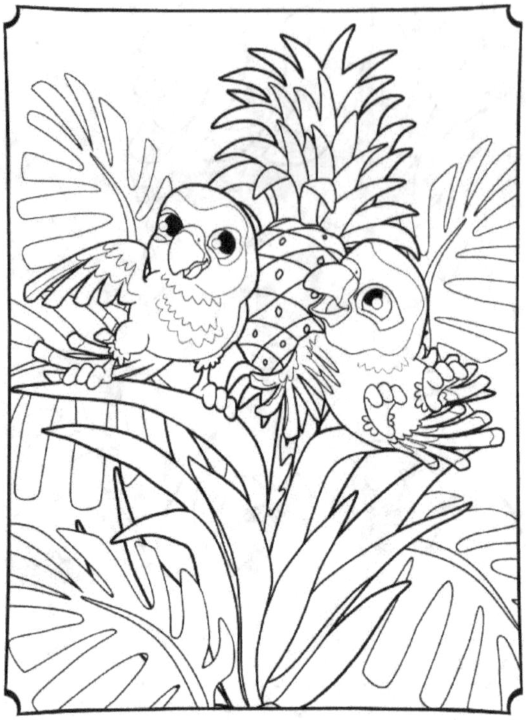

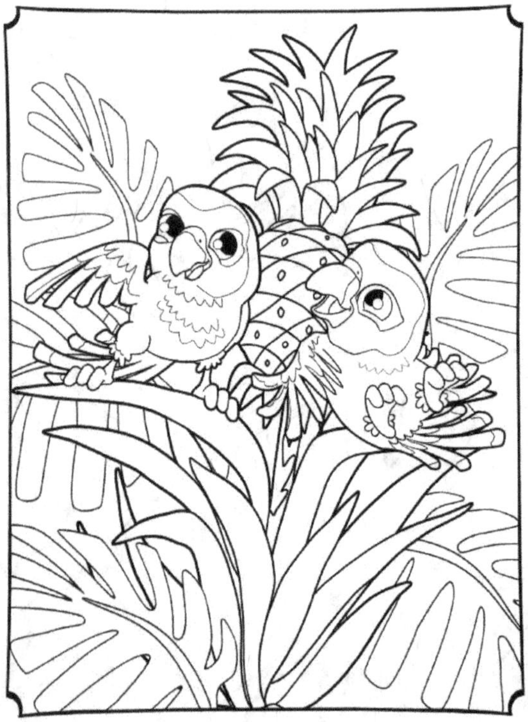

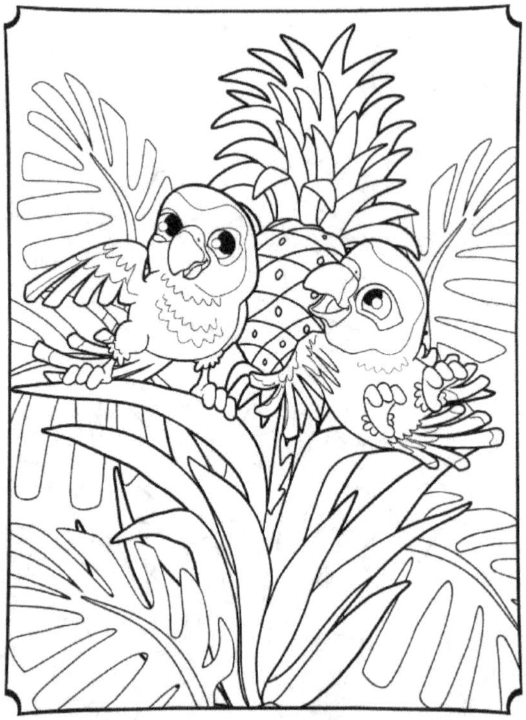

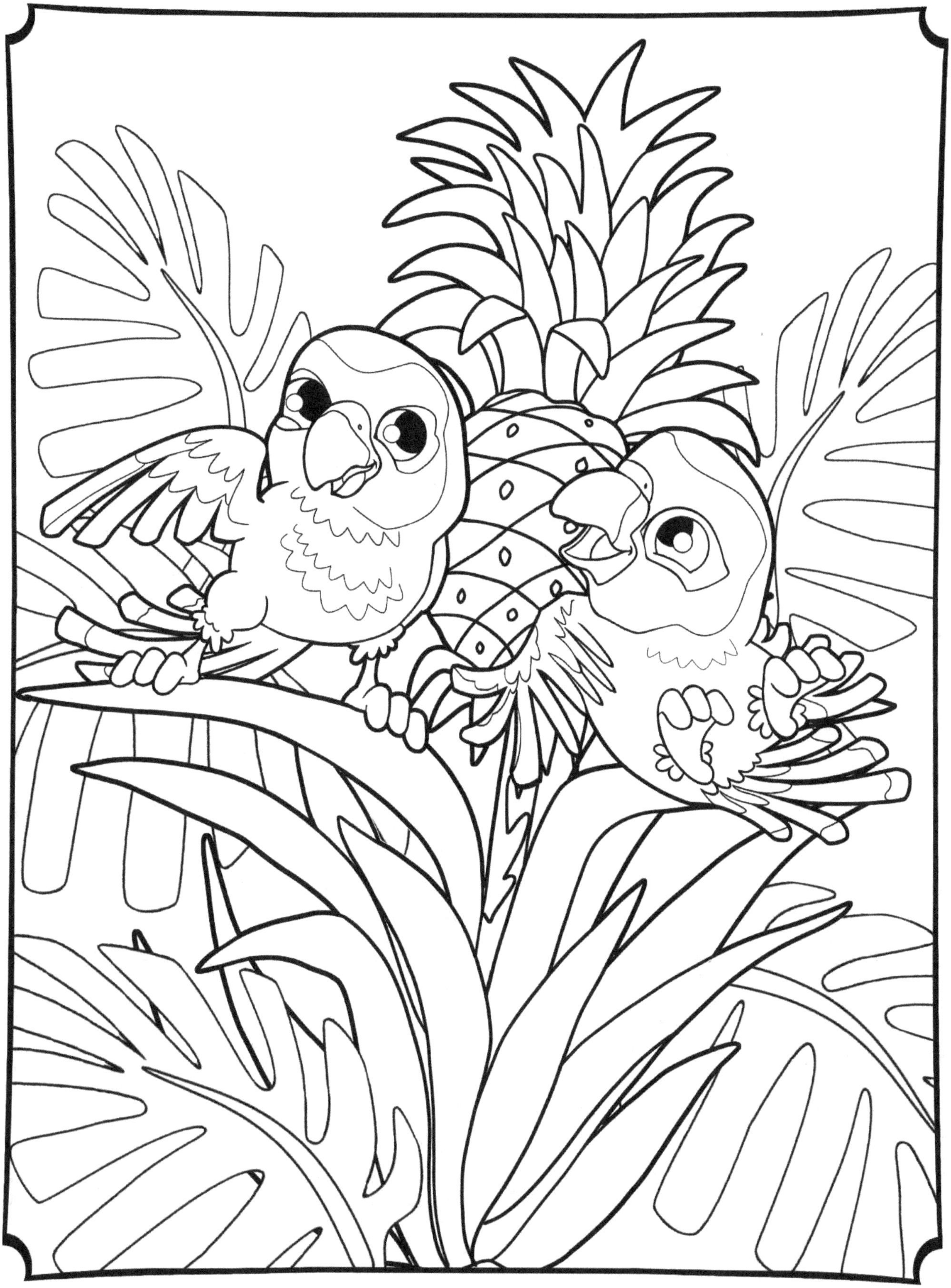

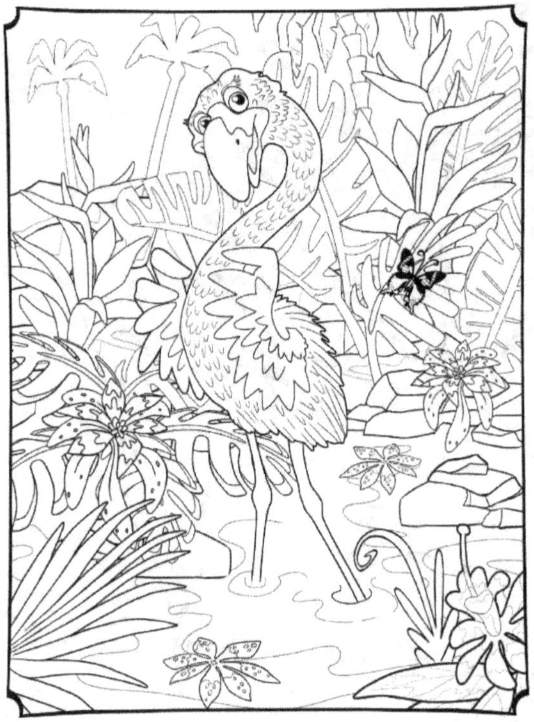
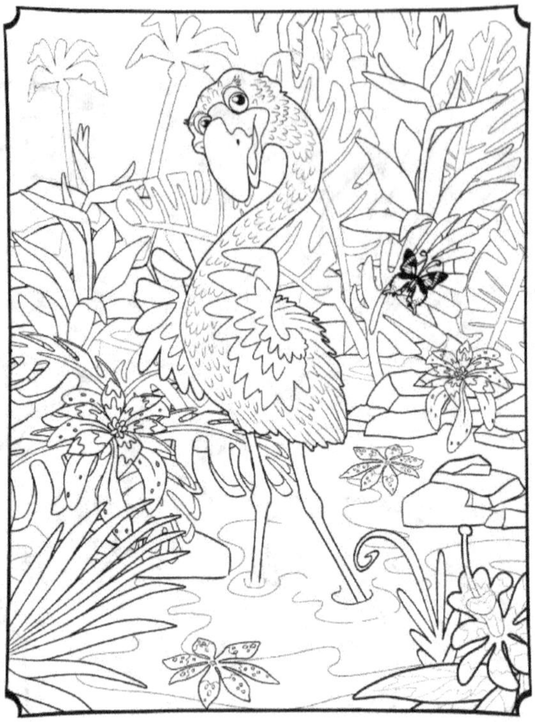
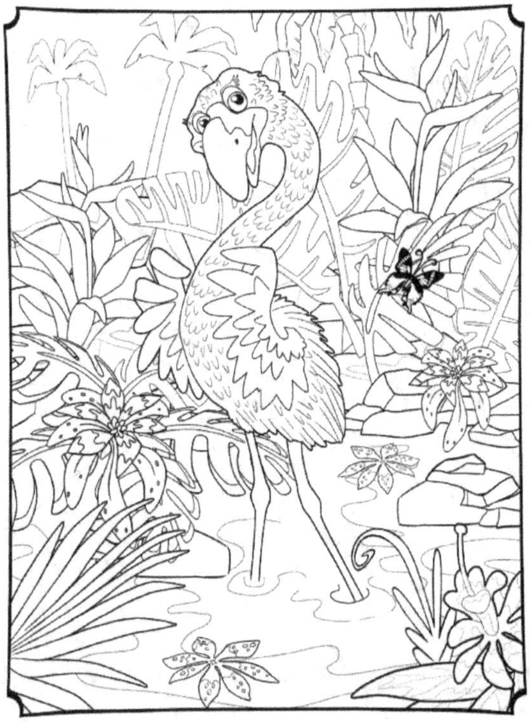
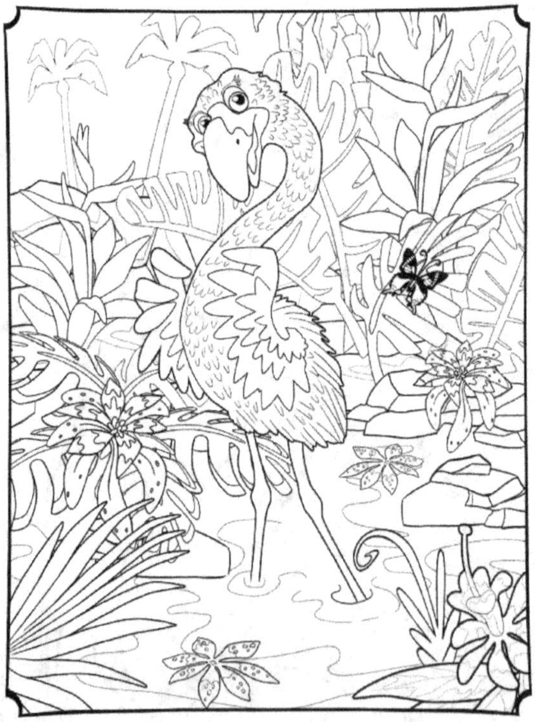

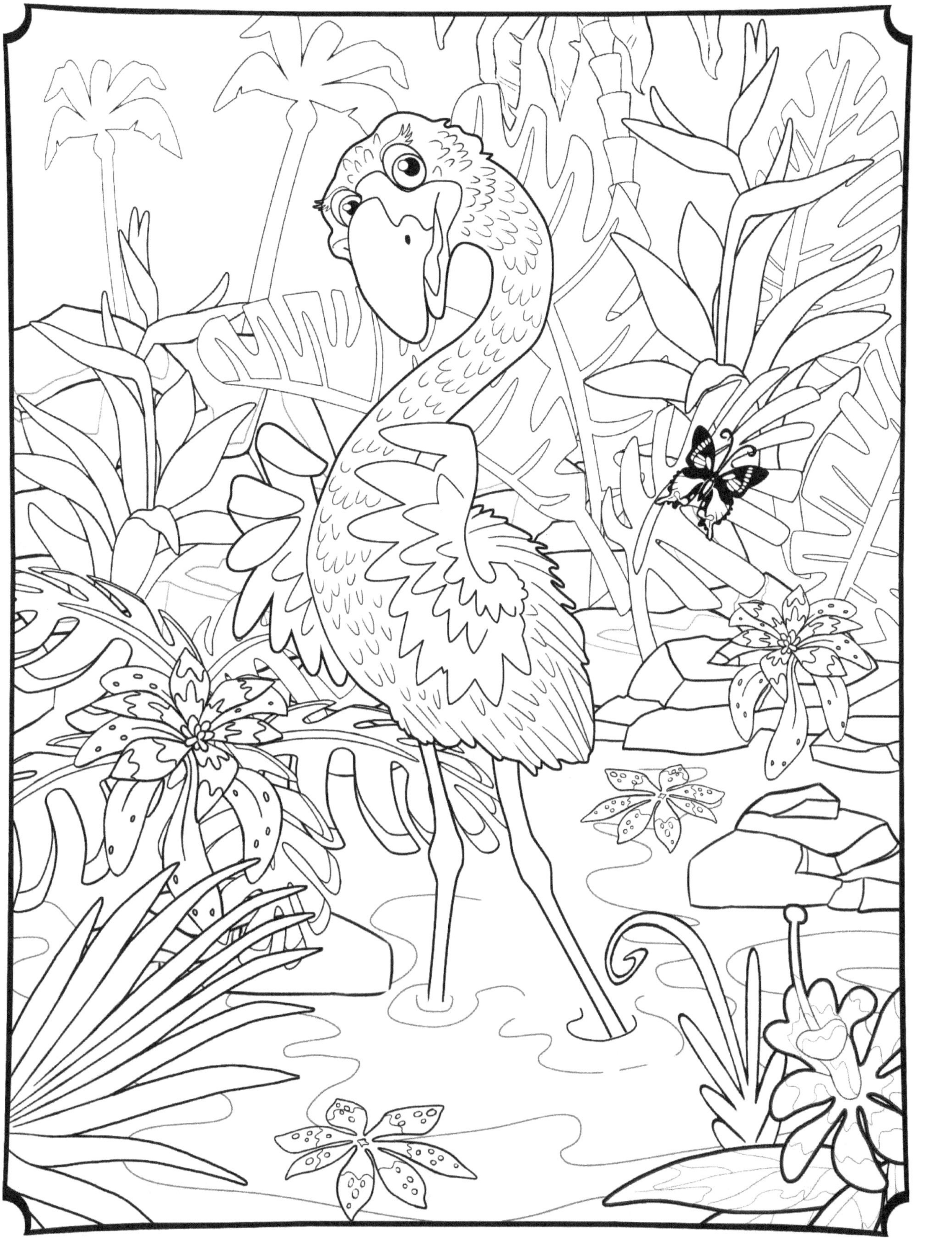

www.ingramcontent.com/pod-product-compliance
Lightning Source LLC
Chambersburg PA
CBHW081453220526
45466CB00008B/2626